# Arabic Verbs and Essentials of Grammar

a practical guide
to the mastery of Arabic

Jane Wightwick
Mahmoud Gaafar

5/99

Printe

DEMCO

**Editorial Director:** Cindy Krejcsi
**Executive Editor:** Mary Jane Maples
**Editor:** Jim Harmon
**Director, World Languages:** Keith Fry
**Design Manager:** Ophelia M. Chambliss
**Production Manager:** Margo Goia


The authors and the publisher would like to thank the following:

Harrassowitz Verlag for their kind permission to reproduce extracts on
pages 9 and 17 from *A Dictionary of Modern Written Arabic* (Hans Wehr, 1961).

Farouk Mustafa, the Center for Middle Eastern Studies, the University of Chicago,
for his review of the manuscript.

ISBN: 0-8442-4605-0

# Contents

# Part Two: *Essentials of Grammar*

## Appendixes

# Introduction

This book is intended for beginning and intermediate learners of Arabic. You could be studying in a group or by yourself. Either way, you should find this book an essential and accessible introduction to Arabic verbs and grammar and a helpful on-going reference.

We are assuming a basic knowledge of the Arabic script as it is not possible to teach this skill within the parameters of this guide. However, to help you we have also included transliteration throughout, using a simplified system (see Appendix (i), page 126).

A principle of writing this book was to make Arabic grammar more understandable by presenting it in an accessible style and stripping it of the finer detail which can cause confusion to learners. There are comprehensive Arabic grammar books available, but these do not always cater well for the beginning or intermediate learner. *Arabic Verbs and the Essentials of Grammar* aims to fill that gap. This guide covers most of what you will need to know about Arabic verbs during your study of modern Arabic, and also provides a useful summary of the main grammar points.

This is a study aid rather than a course. However, there is progression in the two main parts of the book, or you can simply dip in to brush up on a particular area.

We hope you find this book a useful tool in your study of Arabic.

# 1 The Arabic root system

The key to understanding how Arabic grammar works is in its system of roots. Once you understand how roots work, you can start to identify which are the root letters of a word and understand the patterns they produce. You will then be able to form the different structures following the patterns and use your knowledge to pronounce words correctly and to guess at the meaning of vocabulary.

We can begin by looking at some English words:

necessary
unnecessary
necessitate
necessarily
necessity

As a speaker of English, you can see that these words are connected in meaning. You see the combination of letters "necess" and you know that this word is connected with the meaning of "needing." You can recognize the extra letters on the beginning and end of the word as additional to the meaning: *un-* meaning "not"; the ending *-ity* showing that the word is a noun; *-ly* that it is an adverb, etc.

Now look at these Arabic words:

كتب (*kataba*) he wrote

كتاب (*kitaab*) book

مكتب (*maktab*) office

يكتب (*yaktub*) he writes

كاتب (*kaatib*) writer

Can you spot the three Arabic letters that appear in each of the words on the previous page? You should be able to see that these letters appear in all the words:

  1. ك *(kaaf)*    2. ت *(taa')*    3. ب *(baa')*

(Look at *Appendix (i)* if you need to remind yourself of the Arabic alphabet.)

Notice that the letters appear in the same order in all of the words: the *kaaf* comes first, then the *taa'*, and finally the *baa'*. These three letters, in this order, are the root.

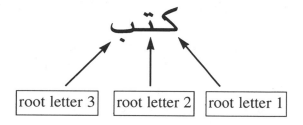

Look back at the previous page again and see if you can spot these three root letters in all the words. Notice that sometimes there are other letters as well as the root letters, but the root letters will always appear in the same sequence.

The root sequence we have looked at (*kaaf, taa', baa'*) is connected with the meaning of "writing." Whenever you see a word with this root, it probably has something to do with writing. The root letters mushroom into many different possible words. For example, when the root letters are put into a particular pattern with the letter *miim* (م) at the front, the meaning becomes "a <u>place</u> of writing," or "a desk/an office":

مكتب *(maktab)*

The vast majority of Arabic words contain three root letters, as in the example above. Much of Arabic grammar is concerned with manipulating the three root letters into different patterns. If you look back at the English words on the first page of this chapter, you will

see that most of the changes take place at the beginning and the end of
the word, leaving the core untouched. Arabic, on the other hand, adds
letters, or combinations of letters, <u>between</u> the root letters, as well as
on the beginning and end. Look at the word for "book" (*kitaab*):

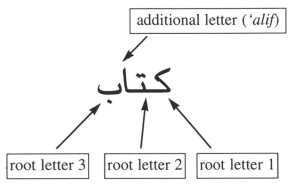

additional letter (*'alif*)

root letter 3    root letter 2    root letter 1

As a symbol to represent the three root letters of any word, Arabic
grammar uses the letters فعل (f/ع/l). So the word for "office" – مَكْتَب
(*maktab*) – is the مَفْعَل (*mafعal*) pattern; i.e., the root letters have *ma* (مـ)
before them, a *sukuun* (ـْ) over the first root letter and a *fatHa* (ـَ) over
the second root letter. In the same way, the word كتابة (*kitaaba*) would
be the فعالة (*fiعaala*) pattern, كُتُب (*kutub*) would be the فُعُل (*fuعul*)
pattern, etc. In the first chapters of the book, we have tried to also use
other common words to illustrate the patterns. However, later we have
introduced more examples using فعل, since this is the convention
understood most widely by both native speakers and Arabists.

You will find the root system very helpful once you have understood
the concept and been introduced to some of the more common patterns.
Native Arabic speakers have an instinctive understanding of how their
language works, but as a learner you will need to approach it more
methodically. Soon you will begin to see the pattern and the shape of
words, and the structure of the language will start to become apparent.

# Using a dictionary

It is worth adding a note about how to use an Arabic dictionary. It is
possible to put Arabic in strict alphabetical order as we do in English,

and this is becoming more common in the age of computerized alphabetization. However, the most widely used dictionaries for learners and native speakers use a system based on the *root* letters of the word. This means all words with the same root letters are grouped together. You will need to try and figure out the root letters of a word before you can look it up in the dictionary. Here is an example from a popular dictionary for learners of Arabic, showing the root كتب (*katab*):

كتب *kataba u* (*katb*, كتبة *kitba*, كتابة *kitāba*) to write, pen [ **basic root** ] down in writing, note down, put down, enter, record, book, register (♦ s.th.); to compose, draw up, indite, draft (♦ s.th.); to bequeath, make over by will (ل ♦ s.th. to s.o.); to prescribe (على ♦ s.th. to s.o.); to foreordain, destine (ل or على ♦ s.th. to s.o.; of God); pass. *kutiba* to be fated, be foreordained, be destined (ل to s.o.) | كتب على نفسه ان to be firmly resolved to ..., make it one's duty to ...; كتب عنه to write from s.o.'s dictation; كتب كتابه (*kitābahū*) to draw up the marriage contract for s.o., marry s.o. (على to) II to make (♦ s.o.) write (♦ s.th.); to form or deploy in squadrons (♦ troops) III to keep up a correspondence, exchange letters, correspond (♦ with s.o.) IV to dictate (♦ ♦ to s.o. s.th.), make write (♦ s.th.) VI to write to each other, exchange letters, keep up a correspondence VII to subscribe VIII to write (♦ s.th.); to copy (♦ s.th.), make a copy (♦ of s.th.); to enter one's name; to subscribe (ل for); to contribute, subscribe (ل ب money to); to be entered, be recorded, be registered X to ask (♦ s.o.) to write (♦ s.th.); to dictate (♦ ♦ to s.o. s.th.), make (♦ s.o.) write (♦ s.th.); to have a copy made (♦ by s.o.)

[ **other words from the same root** ]

كتاب *kitāb* pl. كتب *kutub* piece of writing, record, paper; letter, note, message; document, deed; contract (esp. marriage contract); book; الكتاب the Koran; the Bible | اهل الكتاب *ahl al-k.* the people of the Book, the adherents of a revealed religion, the kitabis, i.e., Christians and Jews; كتاب الزواج *k. az-zawāj* marriage contract; كتاب الطلاق *k. aṭ-ṭalāq* bill of divorce; كتاب تعليمى (*ta'līmī*) textbook; كتاب الاعتماد credentials (*dipl.*); دار الكتب library

كتبى *kutubī* pl. -*ya* bookseller, book-dealer

كتابخانة *kitābḵāna* and كتبخانة *kutubḵāna* library; bookstore

كتاب *kuttāb* pl. كتاتيب *katātīb²* kuttab, Koran school (lowest elementary school)

كتيب *kutayyib* booklet

كتابة *kitāba* (act or practice of) writing; art of writing, penmanship; system of writing, script; inscription; writing, legend; placard, poster; piece of writing, record, paper; secretariat; written amulet, charm; pl. كتابات writings, essays; *kitābatan* in writing | بالكتابة written; بدون كتابة *bi-dūn k.* unwritten, oral; blank; كتابة التاريخ historiography, historical writing; كتابة الدولة *k. ad-daula* (*Maḡr.*) secretariat of state; كتابة عامة (*'āmma*) secretariat general; اسم الكتابة *ism al-k.* pen name, nom de plume; آلة الكتابة typewriter; لغة الكتابة *luḡat al-k.* literary language; ورق الكتابة *waraq al-k.* writing paper

كتابى *kitābī* written, in writing; clerical; literary; scriptural, relating to the revealed Scriptures (Koran, Bible); kitabi, adherent of a revealed religion; the written part (of an examination) | اسلوب كتابى (*uslūb*) literary style; غلطة كتابية (*ḡalṭa*) slip of the pen, clerical error; اعمال كتابية clerical work, office work, desk work; الكمال الكتابى (*kamāl*) literary perfection; لغة كتابية (*luḡa*) literary language; موظف كتابى (*muwaẓẓaf*) clerk, clerical worker (of a government office)

كتيبة *katība* pl. كتائب *katā'ib²* squadron; cavalry detachment; (*Eg.* 1939) battalion, (*Ir.* after 1922) regiment, (later) battalion, (*Syr.*) battalion of armored, cavalry, or motorized, units (*mil.*); (piece of) writing, record, paper, document; written amulet

مكتب *maktab* pl. مكاتب *makātib²* office; bureau; business office; study; school, elementary school; department, agency,

# Part One:
# *Arabic Verbs*

# 2 Regular verbs: The basic tenses

Arabic is relatively straightforward when it comes to tenses. Some languages have many tenses and are very specific about the time of an action and whether or not the action has been completed. Arabic grammar is vague about time and there are only two basic tenses:

• The *past* (or *perfect*) الماضِي

• The *present* (or *imperfect*) المُضارِع

## The Past

In a simple regular verb, the basic past tense will look like this:

كَتَبَ (*kataba*): (he) wrote

شَرِبَ (*shariba*): (he) drank

حَمَلَ (*Hamala*): (he) carried

The three root letters are all followed by a vowel. In most cases this is all *fatHas (kataba/Hamala)*, but sometimes the second vowel is a *KaSra (shariba)*. (In rare cases, the second vowel is a *Damma (u)*, but you can ignore these verbs since you are not likely to see or use them.)

If we take off the final vowel, this هُو ("he/it") part of the verb (third person masculine singular) becomes the base, or *stem* of the past tense. Different endings can be added to this past stem depending on who is carrying out the action (the subject of the verb). So, كَتَبَ (*kataba*) is "he wrote" and كَتَب (*katab*) is the past stem. If we add the ending تُ (*tu*) to the stem, it becomes كَتَبْتُ (*katabtu*) – "I wrote"; if we add نا (*naa*), it becomes كَتَبْنا (*katabnaa*) – "we wrote," etc. Here is a table showing all the endings for the past tense:

|  | **Ending** | **Example** |
|---|---|---|
| *singular* | | |
| أنَا  I | تُ (tu) | كَتَبْتُ (katabtu) |
| أنْتَ  you (masc.*) | تَ (ta) | كَتَبْتَ (katabta) |
| أنْتِ  you (fem.*) | تِ (ti) | كَتَبْتِ (katabti) |
| هُوَ  he/it | ـَ (a) | كَتَبَ (kataba) |
| هِيَ  she/it | ـَتْ (at) | كَتَبَتْ (katabat) |
| *plural* | | |
| نَحْنُ  we | نَا (naa) | كَتَبْنَا (katabnaa) |
| أنْتُمْ  you (masc. pl) | تُمْ (tum) | كَتَبْتُمْ (katabtum) |
| أنْتُنَّ  you (fem. pl) | تُنَّ (tunna) | كَتَبْتُنَّ (katabtunna) |
| هُمْ  they (masc.) | **وا** (uu) | كَتَبُوا (katabuu) |
| هُنَّ  they (fem.) | نَ (na) | كَتَبْنَ (katabna) |

* For an explanation of masculine and feminine genders, see page 107.
** An extra *'alif* (l) is written after the waaw (و) but is *silent*.

Note that you will not meet or need the feminine plurals as often as the masculine plurals. This is because you only use the feminine plural if all the people in a group are female. If the group is mixed male and female, the masculine is used. Therefore, this form is the most important to learn and become familiar with in the first place. There are also different endings for two people (the dual). To make it easier to absorb the basics first, an explanation of the dual and its associated verb endings has been separated. Refer to Chapters 17 and 28 for an explanation of the dual and associated endings if you need it.

You do not have to use the personal pronouns (he, she, etc.) before the verb as you do in English. If you see an Arabic sentence like this:

كَتَبَت رِسالة لأُمِّهَا.   (She) wrote a letter to her mother.

you can tell it is "she" because of the ending of the verb (*katabat*). The sentence could be more specific and say exactly <u>who</u> wrote the letter (the subject of the verb). Then you would see:

كَتَبَت فاطمة رِسالة لأُمِّهَا.   Fatma wrote a letter to her mother.

Notice that in written Arabic the subject (Fatma) usually comes after the verb (wrote). More explanation of word order can be found in Chapter 11.


# The Present

The present is used for an action (or state) which is still going on (unfinished). Whereas the past is formed by adding endings to a stem, the present adds letters on the beginning *and* end of a different present stem to show the subject of the verb. Look first at the present verb below. These letters on the beginning and end are underlined in the third column. Can you identify the stem that appears throughout?


*singular*

| أَنا I | أَكْتُبُ | <u>'a</u>ktub(<u>u</u>*) |
|---|---|---|
| أَنتَ you (masc.) | تَكْتُبُ | <u>ta</u>ktub(<u>u</u>*) |
| أَنتِ you (fem.) | تَكْتُبِينَ | <u>ta</u>ktub<u>iina</u> |
| هُوَ he/it | يَكْتُبُ | <u>ya</u>ktub(<u>u</u>*) |
| هِيَ she/it | تَكْتُبُ | <u>ta</u>ktub(<u>u</u>*) |

* The final ending *(u)* on some of the verbs above has been put in parentheses because it is not usually pronounced.

*plural*

| | | |
|---|---|---|
| نَحْنُ  we | نَكْتُبُ | <u>na</u>ktub(<u>u</u>) |
| أَنْتُمْ  you (masc. pl) | تَكْتُبُونَ | <u>ta</u>ktub<u>uuna</u> |
| أَنْتُنَّ  you (fem. pl) | تَكْتُبْنَ | <u>ta</u>ktub<u>na</u> |
| هُمْ  they (masc.) | يَكْتُبُونَ | <u>ya</u>ktub<u>uuna</u> |
| هُنَّ  they (fem.) | يَكْتُبْنَ | <u>ya</u>ktub<u>na</u> |

If you look at the table, you can see that the present stem — which appears in all the examples — is كْتُبـ *(ktub):* the three root letters *k/t/b*, with no vowel after the first letter and a *Damma* ( ـُ ) after the second.

The different letters added on the beginning and end *(prefixes* and *suffixes)* are arranged around this present stem to show the subject of the verb. For example:

$$ \text{يَكْتُبُونَ} = \text{وُنَ} + \text{كْتُبـ} + \text{يَـ} \qquad \longleftarrow \text{(Read this way.)} $$

| *yaktubuuna*<br>(they write) | = | suffix *(uuna)* | + | stem *(ktub)* | + | prefix *(ya)* |
|---|---|---|---|---|---|---|

We can apply the same principle to another verb:

$$ \text{تَجْلِسِينَ} = \text{يِنَ} + \text{جْلِسـ} + \text{تَـ} $$

| *tajlisiina*<br>(you [fem.] sit) | = | suffix *(iina)* | + | stem *(jlis)* | + | prefix *(ta)* |
|---|---|---|---|---|---|---|

The present is used for both continuous and habitual actions or states, where in English we might use a different tense:

يَلْعَب الأَطْفال الكُرة يَوْم الجُمْعة.

The children <u>play</u> football on Friday(s).

يَجْلِس صَدِيقكَ في مَقْعَدي!

Your friend <u>is sitting</u> in my chair!

As with the past, the vowel on the second root letter varies in the present. If the middle vowel on the past is a *kasra*, then it usually changes to a *fatHa* in the present:

shariba   شَرِب   (he drank)
yashrab   يَشْرَب   (he drinks)

However, the majority of verbs have *fatHa* as the middle vowel of the past and, for these verbs, there is no rule to follow in the present. If you need to know the vowel, you can look in a dictionary where you will find the middle vowel written after the entry:

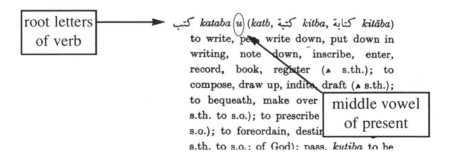

Remember that in most cases the middle vowel will not affect the meaning of the text or your understanding of it. Most Arabic is written without vowels and you will probably learn the more common middle vowels over time. Don't worry too much about this aspect. Native speakers will usually understand you as long as the root letters and the patterns are correct.

## The Future

If you want to talk about the future in Arabic, you also use the present. Often the word سَوْفَ (*sawfa*) or the prefix سَـ (*sa*) are added to the front of the verb to indicate the future.

سَنَذْهَب إلى المَتْحَف المِصْريّ غَدًا.

We are going to the Egyptian museum tomorrow.

سَوْفَ يَزْرَع الفَلَاح البَطاطِس في الخَريف.

The farmer will plant potatoes in the Fall.

# Summary of basic tenses

- There are only two basic tenses in Arabic:
    the past
    the present

- The past stem is formed from the three root letters with a *fatHa* after the first root and a *fatHa* (or sometimes a *kasra*) after the second root letter (*katab/sharib*). Endings are added to the stem to show the subject of the verb.

- The present stem is formed from the three root letters with a vowel after the second (*ktub/shrab/jlis*). Prefixes and endings are added to the stem to show the subject of the verb.

- The future may be made by adding سَوْفَ (*sawfa*) or سَـ (*sa*) to the present.

# 3 Irregular verbs: introduction

Irregular verbs can be defined as verbs that act differently from the basic patterns in all or some cases. Unfortunately for the learner, Arabic has many irregular verbs (although some are more irregular than others!) These fall into three categories and include some of the most common verbs:

- Verbs with *waaw* (و) or *yaa'* (ي) as one of the root letters
- Verbs with *hamza* (ء) as one of the root letters
- *Doubled* verbs, where the second and third letters of the root are the same

The first category is the most common, and verbs in this category also display the most irregularities.

To help you remember the irregular verbs, we have chosen common verbs in each category to illustrate the patterns in which they appear. The verbs you see in the tables and examples in the following chapters are those you will probably encounter on a regular basis and will need to communicate in Arabic. By studying the way they work and meeting them frequently in spoken and written Arabic, these verbs should help to establish the irregular patterns in your mind.

The irregular verbs are covered first in the basic tenses (see Chapter 2 for a review of these tenses). Later chapters cover the various forms and variations. If you need to access this information immediately, go straight to the relevant chapter which will show you how each type of irregular verb behaves in these circumstances. If you want a general overview, work your way more systematically through the chapters in

# 4 Irregular verbs: Verbs with *waaw* or *yaa'* as a root letter

*Waaw* (و) and *yaa'* (ي) are often called *weak letters*, and the verbs they contain called *weak verbs*. These letters do not have a strong sound, unlike letters such as *baa'* (ب) or *kaaf* (ك), and often drop out of words or become vowel sounds when put into the various patterns.

Weak verbs are the largest category of irregular verbs. They can be subdivided into three types depending on which of the root letters is affected:

- Verbs with *waaw* or *yaa'* as the <u>first</u> root letter (*assimilated* verbs)
- Verbs with *waaw* or *yaa'* as the <u>second</u> root letter (*hollow* verbs)
- Verbs with *waaw* or *yaa'* as the <u>third</u> root letter (*defective* verbs)

## *Waaw* or *yaa'* as first root letter

This is one of the simplest irregular patterns.

- Verbs with *yaa'* as the first root letter are rare and almost completely regular. The only significant irregularity is dealt with in Chapter 10 (Derived forms VIII–X).

- Verbs with *waaw* as the first root letter are regular in the past (perfect) tense:

وَجَدْنا عِلّة في البَرْنامَج.

We found a bug (flaw) in the program.

وَعَدَت الحُكومة بِتَخْفيض الضَّرائِب بَعْد الانْتِخابات.

The government promised a reduction in taxes after the elections.

وَصَلُوا إلى شيكاغو بالطائِرة.

They arrived in Chicago by airplane.

In the present, the first root letter almost always drops out completely:

يَصِل (*yaSil*)  he arrives (from the root وصل)

يَجِدُون (*yajiduuna*)  they find  (from the root وجد)

تَضَع (*taDaε*)  she puts  (from the root وضع)

Compare this to the regular form of the present يَكْتُب (*yaktub*). In the assimilated verb, the first root letter has disappeared altogether from the stem, leaving just the second and third root letters (*Sil/jid/Daε*).

The table below shows more fully the present tense for the verb وَصَل/يَصِل (to arrive):

*singular*

| أَنا I | أَصِلُ | 'aSil(u) |
|---|---|---|
| أَنْتَ you (masc.) | تَصِلُ | taSil(u) |
| أَنْتِ you (fem.) | تَصِلينَ | taSiliina |
| هُوَ he/it | يَصِلُ | yaSil(u) |
| هِيَ she/it | تَصِلُ | taSil(u) |

*plural*

| | | |
|---|---|---|
| نَحْنُ we | نَصِلُ | <u>na</u>Sil(<u>u</u>) |
| أَنْتُمْ you (masc. pl) | تَصِلُونَ | <u>ta</u>Sil<u>uu</u>na |
| أَنْتُنَّ you (fem. pl) | تَصِلْنَ | <u>ta</u>Sil<u>na</u> |
| هُم they (masc.) | يَصِلُونَ | <u>ya</u>Sil<u>uu</u>na |
| هُنَّ they (fem.) | يَصِلْنَ | <u>ya</u>Sil<u>na</u> |

# Waaw or yaa' as second root letter

This group of verbs contains some of the most commonly used verbs in the Arabic language. They are called *hollow* verbs because the second (middle) root letter is often replaced by a long or short vowel.

## Hollow verbs in the past

In the past tense, all hollow verbs have a long *aa* sound ( ا ) instead of the middle root letter for هو (he/it), هي (she/it) and هم (they):

كَانَ (*kaana* : "he/it was") from the root: كون
زَارَتْ (*zaarat* : "she visited") from the root: زور
بَاعُوا (*baaع uu* : "they sold") from the root: بيع
طَارَ (*Taara*: "he/it flew") from the root: طير

The other parts of the verb have a short vowel instead of the middle root letter (see separate chapter for dual verbs). This is usually a *Damma* if the middle root letter is a *waaw*, and a *kasra* if it is a *yaa'*:

كُنْتُ (*kuntu*: "I was") from the root: كون
زُرْنَا (*zurnaa*: "we visited") from the root: زور
بِعْتُمْ (*biع tum* : "you [pl.] sold") from the root: بيع
طِرْتِ (*Tirti*: "you [fem.] flew") from the root: طير

كانَ مَريضًا.

He was ill.

طارَت الطائرة فَوقَ الجِبال.

The airplane flew over the mountains.

هَلْ بِعتُم بَيْتكُمْ في نيو يورك؟

Have you sold your house in New York?

زُرْنَا المَتْحَف أمس.

We visited the museum yesterday.

This table summarizes the past tense for hollow verbs:

|  | **Verbs with *waaw*** | **Verbs with *yaa'*** |
|---|---|---|
| *singular* | | |
| أنا I | زُرْتُ (zurtu) | طِرْتُ (Tirtu) |
| أنْتَ you (masc.) | زُرْتَ (zurta) | طِرْتَ (Tirta) |
| أنْتِ you (fem.) | زُرْتِ (zurti) | طِرْتِ (Tirti) |
| هُوَ he/it | زارَ (zaara) | طارَ (Taara) |
| هِيَ she/it | زارَتْ (zaarat) | طارَتْ (Taarat) |
| *plural* | | |
| نَحْنُ we | زُرْنَا (zurnaa) | طِرْنَا (Tirnaa) |
| أنتُمْ you (masc. pl) | زُرْتُمْ (zurtum) | طِرْتُمْ (Tirtum) |
| أنتُنَّ you (fem. pl) | زُرْتُنَّ (zurtunna) | طِرْتُنَّ (Tirtunna) |
| هُم they (masc.) | زارُوا (zaaruu) | طارُوا (Taaruu) |
| هُنَّ they (fem.) | زُرْنَ (zurna) | طِرْنَ (Tirna) |

* See next page for exceptions.

There are a few hollow verbs that behave in the past like verbs with *yaa'* as the middle root letter, but which actually have *waaw* in the middle. By far the most common verb to remember is the verb "to sleep," from the root letters نوم:

نَامَتْ في سَرير أُمّها.
She slept in her mother's bed.

نِمْتُ حَتَّى الصَّبَاح.
I slept until morning.

From the table on page 23, you might have noticed that there is a short vowel in the middle of hollow verbs when there is a sukuun ( ֹ) over the <u>third</u> root letter. This is a general rule for hollow verbs and is worth remembering as it works for all types, tenses, and forms of hollow verbs:

- **Sukuun** over third root letter of regular verb = **short vowel** in the middle of irregular hollow verb
- **Vowel** over third root letter of regular verb = **long vowel** in the middle of irregular hollow verb

## Hollow verbs in the present

In the present tense, hollow verbs also follow the rules highlighted above. Sine the present tense usually has a vowel after the third root letter (even if this is not always pronounced), this means that hollow verbs in this tense are characterised mainly by a long vowel in the middle. The difference is that, whereas in the past the long vowel in the middle is always a long *aa* (*kaana*), in the present it is a long *ii* if the second root letter is a *yaa'* and usually a long *uu* if the second root letter is a *waaw*:

يَزُورُ (*yazuur(u)*: "he visits") from the root: زور
يَبِيعُونَ (*yabiiɛ uuna*: "they sell") from the root: بيع

Verbs like نوم (see above) are the exception since they have a long *aa* the middle of the present:

يَنَامُ (*yanaamu*) he sleeps
يَنَامُونَ (*yanaamuuna*) they sleep

Here is a complete table and some examples showing the three
different types of hollow verb in the present. Pay the most attention to
learning the first two types. The third type has been included mainly
for recognition. Notice that only the less common feminine plurals
have a sukuun over the third root letter and a short vowel in the
middle. As in the past, this vowel depends on the middle root letter.

| | Most verbs with *waaw* | Verbs with *yaa'* | Verbs like نوم |
|---|---|---|---|
| *singular* | | | |
| أَنَا | أَزُورُ ('azuur[u]) | أَطِيرُ ('aTiir[u]) | أَنَامُ ('anaam[u]) |
| أَنْتَ | تَزُورُ (tazuur[u]) | تَطِيرُ (taTiir[u]) | تَنَامُ (tanaam[u]) |
| أَنْتِ | تَزُورِينَ (tazuuriina) | تَطِيرِينَ (taTiiriina) | تَنَامِينَ (tanaamiina) |
| هُوَ | يَزُورُ (yazuur[u]) | يَطِيرُ (yaTiir[u]) | يَنَامُ (yanaam[u]) |
| هِيَ | تَزُورُ (tazuur[u]) | تَطِيرُ (taTiir[u]) | تَنَامُ (tanaam[u]) |
| *plural* | | | |
| نَحْنُ | نَزُورُ (nazuur[u]) | نَطِيرُ (naTiir[u]) | نَنَامُ (nanaam[u]) |
| أَنْتُمْ | تَزُورُونَ (tazuuruuna) | تَطِيرُونَ (taTiiruuna) | تَنَامُونَ (tanaamuuna) |
| أَنْتُنَّ | تَزُرْنَ (tazurna) | تَطِرْنَ (taTirna) | تَنَمْنَ (tanamna) |
| هُم | يَزُورُونَ (yazuuruuna) | يَطِيرُونَ (yaTiiruuna) | يَنَامُونَ (yanaamuuna) |
| هُنَّ | يَزُرْنَ (yazurna) | يَطِرْنَ (yaTirna) | يَنَمْنَ (yanamna) |

زَبوننا الرَئيسِيّ يَزُور مكْتَبنا كُلّ شَهْر.

Our major client visits our office every month.

نَبيع المَحْصُول لتُجَّار الجُمْلة.

We sell the crop to wholesalers.

أَنَام كُلّ يَوْم الساعة الثَانية عَشُرَة.

I go to sleep every day at twelve o'clock.

# Waaw or yaa' as third root letter

This group of verbs is sometimes called *defective* verbs. There are three main types:

- Verbs with *waaw* as the last root letter.
- Verbs with *yaa'* as the last root letter and *fatHa* as the middle vowel in the past
- Verbs with *yaa'* as the last root letter and *kasra* as the middle vowel in the past

In the past tense, the first two types are reasonably regular. Only the parts of the verb for هو (he/it), هي (she/it) and هم (they) are irregular:

From the root شكو:
شَكا (*shakaa*: "he complained")
شَكَتْ (*shakat*: "she complained")
شَكَوْا (*shakaw*: "they complained")

From the root مشي:
مَشَى (*mashaa*: "he walked")
مَشَتْ (*mashat*: "she walked")
مَشَوْا (*mashaw*: "they walked")

All of the irregular parts of these two types are pronounced the same. The only difference is the spelling of شَكا (*shakaa*) with a final *'alif*, and مشى (*mashaa*) with a final *yaa'* (without the dots). (Look at Appendix (i) if you want to know more details about this final *yaa'* which is pronounced *aa* and known as *'alif maqsuura*.) The differences between these two types of verbs are more apparent in the regular parts of the past:

شَكَوْتُ (*shakawtu* : "I complained") from the root: شكو

مَشَيْنَا (*mashaynaa* : "we walked") from the root: مشي

رَمَيْتَ (*ramayta* : "you threw") from the root: رمي

رَجَوْتُمْ (*rajawtum*: "you [pl.] requested/implored") from the root: رجو

Most defective verbs follow one of the two patterns above. However, there are some verbs with *yaa'* as the last root letter and *kasra* as the middle vowel that follow a different pattern. Two common examples are the verbs نَسِيَ (*nasiya* – to forget) and لَقِيَ (*laqiya* – to meet). These verbs have a long *ii* in many parts of the past tense, e.g. نَسِيتُ (*nasiitu*) – "I forgot."

The following table summarizes the past tense for all three main types of defective verbs:

| | *defective type 1* (شكا: to complain) | *defective type 2* (مشى: to walk) | *defective type 3* (نسي: to forget) |
|---|---|---|---|
| *singular* | | | |
| أَنَا | شَكَوْتُ (shakawtu) | مَشَيْتُ (mashaytu) | نَسِيتُ (nasiitu) |
| أَنْتَ | شَكَوْتَ (shakawta) | مَشَيْتَ (mashayta) | نَسِيتَ (nasiita) |
| أَنْتِ | شَكَوْتِ (shakawti) | مَشَيْتِ (mashayti) | نَسِيتِ (nasiiti) |
| هُوَ | شَكَا (shakaa) | مَشَى (mashaa) | نَسِيَ (nasiya) |
| هِيَ | شَكَتْ (shakat) | مَشَتْ (mashat) | نَسِيَتْ (nasiyat) |

| | defective type 1<br>(شكا: to complain) | defective type 2<br>(مشى: to walk) | defective type 3<br>(نسي: to forget) |
|---|---|---|---|
| *plural* | | | |
| نَحْنُ | شَكَوْنَا (shakawnaa) | مَشَيْنَا (mashaynaa) | نَسِينَا (nasiinaa) |
| أَنْتُمْ | شَكَوْتُمْ (shakawtum) | مَشَيْتُمْ (mashaytum) | نَسِيتُمْ (nasiitum) |
| أَنْتُنَّ | شَكَوْتُنَّ (shakawtunna) | مَشَيْتُنَّ (mashaytunna) | نَسِيتُنَّ (nasiitunna) |
| هُم | شَكَوْا (shakaw) | مَشَوْا (mashaw) | نَسُوا (nasuu) |
| هُنَّ | شَكَوْنَ (shakawna) | مَشَيْنَ (mashayna) | نَسِينَ (nasiina) |

Here are the three types of defective verbs in the present tense:

| | defective type 1<br>(يشكو: to complain) | defective type 2<br>(يمشي: to walk) | defective type 3<br>(ينسى: to forget) |
|---|---|---|---|
| *singular* | | | |
| أَنا | أَشْكُو ('ashkuu) | أَمْشِي ('amshii) | أَنْسَى ('ansaa) |
| أَنْتَ | تَشْكُو (tashkuu) | تَمْشِي (tamshii) | تَنْسَى (tansaa) |
| أَنْتِ | تَشْكِينَ (tashkiina*) | تَمْشِينَ (tamshiina*) | تَنْسَيْنَ (tansayna) |
| هُوَ | يَشْكُو (yashkuu) | يمْشِي (yamshii) | يَنْسَى (yansaa) |
| هِيَ | تَشْكُو (tashkuu) | تَمْشِي (tamshii) | تَنْسَى (tansaa) |
| *plural* | | | |
| نَحْنُ | نَشْكُو (nashkuu) | نمْشِي (namshii) | نَنْسَى (nansaa) |
| أَنْتُمْ | تَشْكُونَ (tashkuuna*) | تَمْشُونَ (tamshuuna*) | تَنْسَوْنَ (tansawna) |
| أَنْتُنَّ | تَشْكُونَ (tashkuuna) | تَمْشِينَ (tamshiina) | تَنْسَيْنَ (tansayna) |
| هُم | يَشْكُونَ (yashkuuna*) | يَمْشُونَ (yamshuuna*) | يَنْسَوْنَ (yansawna) |
| هُنَّ | يَشْكُونَ (yashkuuna) | يمْشِينَ (yamshiina) | يَنْسَيْنَ (yansayna) |

*Notice that the weak third root letter drops out altogether in these cases.*

Notice that defective verbs in the present tense can usually be spotted because they have a long vowel instead of the third root letter. In type 1 this is a long *uu* (*yashkuu*); in type 2 a long *ii* (*yamshii*) and in type 3 a long *aa* (*yansaa*) — but note this is written with *'alif maqsura*, see Appendix (i). Some of the changes that happen are not very logical and can be difficult to remember. Concentrate on the most common parts first. Leave the other parts (e.g., feminine plural) until you feel confident with the basic patterns.

# Summary of weak verbs

- Weak verbs are those which have *waaw* (و) or *yaa'* (ي) as one of the root letters.

- There are three types of weak verb:
  Verbs with *waaw* or *yaa'* as the <u>first</u> root letter (*assimilated* verbs)
  Verbs with *waaw* or *yaa'* as the <u>second</u> root letter (*hollow* verbs)
  Verbs with *waaw* or *yaa'* as the <u>third</u> root letter (*defective* verbs)

- *Assimilated* verbs are mainly regular except the first root letter almost always drops out in the present tense.

- *Hollow* verbs have a vowel in the middle instead of the second root letter. This is a *short* vowel if the <u>third</u> root letter has a sukuun ( ٰ ) over it, and a *long* vowel if it does not.

- *Defective* verbs are characterized by a long vowel *(aa/uu/ii)* or a diphthong *(ay/aw)* instead of the third root letter, but do not always behave predictably. Each pattern should be learned individually.

# 5 Irregular verbs: Doubled verbs

Doubled verbs are those where the third root letter is the same as the second root letter. They are one of the simplest forms of irregular verbs to master. The general rule is similar to the rule for hollow verbs and is dependent on the vowel over the <u>third</u> root letter:

> • **Sukuun** over third root letter of regular verb =
>   second and third root letters **written separately** in doubled verb
> • **Vowel** over third root letter of regular verb =
>   second and third root letters **written together** in doubled verb

For example, the past tense pattern كَتَبُوا (*katabuu* – they wrote) has the vowel *Damma* (ُ) over the third root letter. So, in a doubled verb, the second and third root letters would be written together with a *shadda* (ّ) in this pattern:

شَكُّوا (*shakkuu* : "they doubted") from the root: شك
رَدَّتْ (*raddat* : "she replied") from the root: رد

However, the past tense pattern كَتَبْنَا (*katabnaa* – "we wrote") has a *sukuun* (ْ) over the third root letter. So in a doubled verb, the second and third root letters would be written separately in this pattern:

شَكَكْنَا (*shakaknaa* : "we doubted")
رَدَدْتُ (*radadtu* : "I replied")

The same rules apply to the present tense (look back at Chapter 2 if you need to remind yourself of the patterns for regular verbs).

As most parts of the present tense have a vowel after the third root letter, this means that you will see the root letters in a doubled verb written together in most cases. In addition, the middle vowel of the present tense (mostly *Damma* in doubled verbs) shifts back over the first root letter:

أَوَدّ أَنْ أَشْكُرَكَ عَلَى خِطَابِكَ الأَخِير.

I'd like to thank you for your last letter.

سَأَمُدُّكَ بِالمَعْلُومَات الَتِي طَلَبْتَها فَوْرًا.

I will send you the information you requested immediately.

Here is a table summarizing the past and present patterns for doubled verbs. A good exercise is to cover the column showing the doubled verb and see if you can predict the pattern according to the rules on page 30.

| *singular* | Doubled verbs in the past | Doubled verbs in the present |
|---|---|---|
| أَنَا I | رَدَدْتُ radadtu | أَرُدّ 'arudd(u) |
| أَنْتَ you (masc.) | رَدَدْتَ radadta | تَرُدّ tarudd(u) |
| أَنْتِ you (fem.) | رَدَدْتِ radadti | تَرُدِّينَ taruddiina |
| هُوَ he/it | رَدَّ radda | يَرُدّ yarudd(u) |
| هِيَ she/it | رَدَّتْ raddat | تَرُدّ tarudd(u) |

| *plural* | | |
|---|---|---|
| نَحْنُ we | رَدَدْنَا radadnaa | نَرُدّ narudd(u) |
| أَنْتُمْ you (masc. pl) | رَدَدْتُمْ radadtum | تَرُدُّونَ tarudduuna |
| أَنْتُنَّ you (fem. pl) | رَدَدْتُنَّ radadtunna | تَرْدُدْنَ tardudna |
| هُم they (masc.) | رَدُّوا radduu | يَرُدُّونَ yarudduuna |
| هُنَّ they (fem.) | رَدَدْنَ radadna | يَرْدُدْنَ yardudna |

A final cautionary note about doubled verbs: many spoken dialects treat these verbs in the past like verbs with *yaa'* as the final root letter (see Defective verbs, Chapter 4). This means that many native speakers would say رَدَيْنا (*radaynaa*) for "we replied" rather than the grammatically correct رَدَدْنا (*radadnaa*). In fact, this is also a common written error among native speakers. This can be confusing to a learner and is worth a special mention.

# Summary of doubled verbs

- Doubled verbs have the same second and third root letter.

- There are simple rules governing the way these verbs behave: the doubled root letters are written separately if the <u>third</u> root letter has a sukuun ( ّ ) over it, and written together if it does not.

# 6 Irregular verbs: Verbs with *hamza*

The *hamza* can be an enigmatic letter. The nearest analogy in English is the apostrophe. In both cases there is uncertainty as to when and how to use it, even among native speakers. The apostrophe causes more errors in English than virtually anything else and the *hamza* probably holds this dubious distinction in Arabic. Whereas in English we ask ourselves: "Should the apostrophe come before the *s* or after the *s*?," in Arabic the question becomes: "Which letter should carry the *hamza*?" When you review this chapter, it is always worth reminding yourself that you are not alone in finding the *hamza* sometimes elusive. Read the general guidelines but be prepared to refer to the tables regularly.

The *hamza* itself is considered a consonant, not a vowel, pronounced as a short glottal stop — see Appendix (i) for more detail on pronunciation. Many verbs have *hamza* as one of the root letters. It can be any of the three root letters and is found in some common verbs.

Like the apostrophe, the rules (such as they exist) for *hamza* are more concerned with where to place it than how to pronounce it. Verbs with *hamza* as one of the root letters are mainly regular. The changes that occur are in the letter that carries the *hamza*.

There are some guidelines for writing *hamza*. The simplest way to predict how a particular pattern will be written is to look at the pattern for regular verbs (see Chapter 2), and then apply the general rules on the following page. Remember that there are exceptions and alternatives. For individual verbs, check the tables in this chapter and in the relevant chapters for derived forms or other patterns.

**General rules for verbs with *hamza* as one of the root letters**

* If the *hamza* is at the beginning of the verb, it is written on an *'alif*:
  أَخَذَ (he took)/ أَكَلُوا (they ate)

* If a pattern means you would need to write two *'alifs,*
  then these are combined as one with a madda sign over it ( آ ),
  pronouned as a long *aa:* آخُذ – *'aakhudh* (I take), instead of أَأْخُذ

* Otherwise, the letter carrying the *hamza* tends to relate to the vowel
  <u>before</u> the *hamza*:
  – *Damma* before *hamza* = *hamza* written on *waaw* (ؤ)
  – *Kasra* before *hamza* = *hamza* written on *yaa'* without dots (ئ or ـئـ)
  – *FatHa* before *hamza* = *hamza* written on *'alif* (أ)

* If the *hamza* has no vowel before it (i.e., the letter before has a
  *sukuun* over it), then the rules above default to the vowel over the
  *hamza* itself: يَسْأَل (he asks)

*Examples:*
قَرَأْنَا مَسْرَحِيّة عَرَبِيّة في الفَصْل.
We read an Arabic play in class.

سَأَلْتُ المُدَرِّس سُؤَالاً عَن المُؤَلِّف .
I asked the teacher a question about the author.

قَالَ إنّ المُؤَلِّف كَتَبَ المسرحيّة في السَبْعينات...
He said that the author wrote the play in the seventies...

...لأنَّه سَئِمَ من عَمَلِهِ في البَنْك.
...because he was fed up with his work in the bank.

Don't worry if these rules seem complicated. In the basic tenses there
are very few other irregularities, and the majority of patterns are
written with the *hamza* on an *'alif*. If you refer to the tables on page
35, you will start to get a feel for how to write these verbs.

Look at the general rules on page 34 in conjunction with the later chapters if you need to find out how the verbs with *hamza* behave in the derived forms or other patterns.

## Past tense

| | Hamza as root 1 (أخذ: to take) | | Hamza as root 2 (سأل: to ask) | | Hamza as root 3 (بَطُؤ: to be slow*) | |
|---|---|---|---|---|---|---|
| *singular* | | | | | | |
| أَنَا | أَخَذْتُ | ('akhadhtu) | سَأَلْتُ | (sa'altu) | بَطُؤْتُ | (baTu'tu) |
| أَنْتَ | أَخَذْتَ | ('akhadhta) | سَأَلْتَ | (sa'alta) | بَطُؤْتَ | (baTu'ta) |
| أَنْتِ | أَخَذْتِ | ('akhadhti) | سَأَلْتِ | (sa'alti) | بَطُؤْتِ | (baTu'ti) |
| هُوَ | أَخَذَ | ('akhadha) | سَأَلَ | (sa'ala) | بَطُؤَ | (baTu'a) |
| هِيَ | أَخَذَتْ | ('akhadhat) | سَأَلَتْ | (sa'alat) | بَطُؤَتْ | (baTu'at) |
| *plural* | | | | | | |
| نَحْنُ | أَخَذْنَا | ('akhadhnaa) | سَأَلْنَا | (sa'alnaa) | بَطُؤْنَا | (baTu'naa) |
| أَنْتُمْ | أَخَذْتُمْ | ('akhadhtum) | سَأَلْتُمْ | (sa'altum) | بَطُؤْتُمْ | (baTu'tum) |
| أَنْتُنَّ | أَخَذْتُنَّ | ('akhadhtunna) | سَأَلْتُنَّ | (sa'altunna) | بَطُؤْتُنَّ | (baTu'tunna) |
| هُم | أَخَذُوا | ('akhadhuu) | سَأَلُوا | (sa'aluu) | بَطُؤُوا | (baTu'uu) |
| هُنَّ | أَخَذْنَ | ('akhadhna) | سَأَلْنَ | (sa'alna) | بَطُؤْنَ | (baTu'na) |

*This verb is one of a very few that have *Damma* as the vowel on the middle root letter (i.e., the ط )in the past. It has been chosen to show how the *hamza* is usually written when preceded by a *Damma*.

## *Present tense*

| | *Hamza as root 1*<br>(يأخذ: to take) | | *Hamza as root 2*<br>(يسأل: to ask) | | *Hamza as root 3*<br>(يبطؤ: to be slow) | |
|---|---|---|---|---|---|---|
| *singular* | | | | | | |
| أنا | آخُذ | ('aakhudh[u]) | أسْأَل | ('as'al[u]) | أبْطُؤ | ('abTu'[u]) |
| أنْتَ | تأخُذ | (ta'khudh[u]) | تسْأَل | (tas'al[u]) | تبْطُؤ | (tabTu'[u]) |
| أنْتِ | تأخُذِينَ | (ta'khudhiina) | تسْأَلِينَ | (tas'aliina) | تبْطُؤِينَ | (tabTu'iina) |
| هُوَ | يأخُذ | (ya'khudh[u]) | يسْأَل | (yas'al[u]) | يبْطُؤ | (yabTu'[u]) |
| هِيَ | تأخُذ | (ta'khudh[u]) | تسْأَل | (tas'al[u]) | تبْطُؤ | (tabTu'[u]) |

| | | | | | | |
|---|---|---|---|---|---|---|
| *plural* | | | | | | |
| نَحْنُ | نأخُذ | (na'khudh[u]) | نسْأَل | (nas'al[u]) | نبْطُؤ | (nabTu'[u]) |
| أنْتُمْ | تأخُذُونَ | (ta'khudhuuna) | تسْأَلُونَ | (tas'aluuna) | تبْطُؤُونَ | (tabTu'uuna) |
| أنْتُنَّ | تأخُذْنَ | (ta'khudhna) | تسْأَلْنَ | (tas'alna) | تبْطُؤْنَ | (tabTu'na) |
| هُم | يأخُذُونَ | (ya'khudhuuna) | يسْأَلُونَ | (yas'aluuna) | يبْطُؤُونَ | (yabTu'uuna) |
| هُنَّ | يأخُذْنَ | (ya'khudhna) | يسْأَلْنَ | (yas'alna) | يبْطُؤْنَ | (yabTu'na) |

Remember that in the present tense the middle vowel will vary, as it does with regular verbs (see page 17). In the case of verbs with *hamza* as the second or third root letter, this could affect the spelling, although a middle *fatHa* with the *hamza* carried by an *'alif* (أ) is by far the most common.

# Summary of verbs with *hamza*

- Irregularities in these verbs are mainly concerned with the script (which letter carries the *hamza*).

- There are some general rules which help to determine how the *hamza* should be written.

- There are also exceptions and alternatives which need to be individually absorbed over time.

# 7 Forms of the verb: Introduction

While Arabic is not rich in tenses, it makes up for this with its system of verb patterns, or *forms*. All the verbs covered in Chapters 1 to 6 have been the basic, or *root*, form of the verb. The Arabic language plays with this root to add subtle variations to the meaning.

If you look at these groups of words in English, you can see they have different but connected meanings:

liquidate
liquefy
liquidize

validate
value
revalue

By adding different endings and prefixes, the meaning is slightly changed. For example, as a native speaker you recognize that the prefix "re-" means "to do something again."

Arabic takes this principle much further with many different patterns that add meaning to the original root form. These *derived* forms are the major way in which Arabic achieves its richness of vocabulary. Look at the following examples, all derived from the same root

قَتَلُوا (*qataluu*) they killed

قَتَّلُوا (*qattaluu*) they massacred ("killed intensely")

قَاتَلُوا (*qaataluu*) they battled ("tried to kill")

تَقَاتَلُوا (*taqaataluu*) they fought each other

All these are different forms of the same root قتل (*q/t/l*). The verb ending associated with "they" in the past (*uu*) stays the same, but different letters have been added between and before the root to add to the original meaning.

There are eight significant derived forms. Some others exist, but are only seen in poetry or archaic texts. Western scholars of Arabic refer to the forms by Latin numbers: form II ("form two"), form III, form IV, etc. However, native speakers will not be familiar with this. They will know them by the <u>present tense</u> of the pattern, using the root فعل (f/ع/l) — see Chapter 1 for more about this. For example, the verb قاتلوا (they battled), shown in the examples earlier, would be referred to as form III by Arabists, but as the pattern يفاعل (*yufaaع il*) by native speakers and Arabic grammarians. In the following chapters, we will refer to the forms by their numbers, with the فعل pattern in brackets.

Most of the forms are connected with certain meanings — such as trying to do something, doing something together, etc. — although sometimes these meanings have strayed over time or have been adopted for a new concept. All the derived forms do not exist for all roots, but most roots have at least one or two forms in general circulation. You will need to look in a dictionary under the root to know exactly which forms exist. In addition, Arabic speakers will sometimes make up new verbs from existing roots, either as a joke or in an effort to be creative or poetic.

Although the derived forms can at first seem complicated, they are in fact a useful aid for the learner. If you recognize a derived pattern and know another word with the same root, you can often take a good guess at the meaning even if you have never seen that particular word before. The next three chapters will show you the derived patterns and meanings connected with them, as well as any differences in how the irregular verbs behave in these forms.

# 8 Derived forms II–IV

The first of the three main groups of derived forms is made up of
forms II (يُفَعِّل – *yufaععil*), III (يُفَاعِل – *yufaaعil*), and IV (يُفْعِل – *yufعil*).

## Characteristics

### Past tense

- Form II is made by doubling the second root letter of the basic verb:

  فَعَلَ (basic verb *faعala*) ➜ فَعَّلَ (form II verb *faععala*)

- Form III is made by adding a long *aa* (ـَا) after the second root letter:

  فَعَلَ (basic verb *faعala*) ➜ فَاعَلَ (form III verb *faaعala*)

- Form IV is formed by adding an *'alif* before the first root letter and a
*sukuun* (ـْ) over it:

  فَعَلَ (basic verb *faعala*) ➜ أَفْعَلَ (form IV verb *'afعala*)

### Present tense

In the present tense, these three forms have a *Damma* (ـُ) as the first
vowel and a *kasra* (ـِ) as the last. Forms II and III have a *fatHa* (ـَ) over
the first root letter. Form IV has a *sukuun* over the first root letter, as in
the past tense:

  Form II: يُفَعِّل (*yufaععil*)
  Form III: يُفَاعِل (*yufaaعil*)
  Form IV: يُفْعِل (*yufعil*)

It is worth noting that forms II, III and IV are the only verb forms that
have a *Damma* as the opening vowel.

# Common meaning patterns

**1.** Forms II and IV can have the meaning of carrying out an action to someone/something else (making a verb *transitive* or *causative*):

يَدْرُس (basic verb *yadrus* – to study)→
يُدَرِّس (form II verb *yudarris* – to teach)

يَسْخُن (basic verb *yaskhun* – to become hot)→
يُسَخِّن (form II verb *yusakhkhin* – to heat ["to make something hot"])

يَخْرُج (basic verb *yakhruj* – to go out)→
يُخْرِج (form IV verb *yukhrij* – to remove/eject ["to take something out"])

Sometimes a root can be put into forms II <u>and</u> IV with the same or almost the same meaning. Watch for the subtle differences, e.g.:

يَعْلَم (basic verb *yaε lam* – to know)→
يُعَلِّم (form II verb *yuε allim* – to instruct), and…
يُعْلِم (form IV verb *yuε lim* – to inform)

**2.** Form II can also give a verb the meaning of doing something intensively and/or repeatedly:

يَقْتُل (basic verb *yaqtul* – to kill)→
يُقَتِّل (form II verb *yuqattil* – to massacre)

يَكْسَر (basic verb *yaksar* – to break)→
يُكَسِّر (form II verb *yukassir* – to smash up)

**3.** Form III often carries the meaning of "doing something with someone else":

يَجْلِس (basic verb *yajlis* – to sit)→
يُجالِس (form III verb *yujaalis* – to sit with [someone])

يَعْمَل (basic verb *yaε mal* – to do)→
يُعامِل (form III verb *yuε aamil* – to treat/deal with [someone])

**4.** Form III can also carry the meaning of "trying to do something":

يَقْتُل (basic verb *yaqtul* – to kill)→

يُقاتِل (form II verb *yuqaatil* – to battle ["to try to kill"])

يَسْبِق (basic verb *yasbiq* – to come before/precede)→

يُسابِق (form III verb *yusaabiq* – to race ["to try to come before"])

In fact, the verb "to try" is itself a form III verb:

يُحاوِل (*yuHaawil*)

Here is a table showing the past and present tenses for these three verb forms, followed by some example sentences:

## Past

| | Form II<br>(*faɛɛala*) | | Form III<br>(*faaɛala*) | | Form IV<br>(*'afɛala*) | |
|---|---|---|---|---|---|---|
| *singular* | | | | | | |
| أنا | دَرَّسْتُ | (darrastu) | سابَقْتُ | (saabaqtu) | أَعْلَمْتُ | ('aɛlamtu) |
| أنْتَ | دَرَّسْتَ | (darrasta) | سابَقْتَ | (saabaqta) | أَعْلَمْتَ | ('aɛlamta) |
| أنْتِ | دَرَّسْتِ | (darrasti) | سابَقْتِ | (saabaqti) | أَعْلَمْتِ | ('aɛlamti) |
| هُوَ | دَرَّسَ | (darrasa) | سابَقَ | (saabaqa) | أَعْلَمَ | ('aɛlama) |
| هِيَ | دَرَّسَتْ | (darrasat) | سابَقَتْ | (saabaqat) | أَعْلَمَتْ | ('aɛlamat) |

| | | | | | | |
|---|---|---|---|---|---|---|
| *plural* | | | | | | |
| نَحْنُ | دَرَّسْنا | (darrasnaa) | سابَقْنا | (saabaqnaa) | أَعْلَمْنا | ('aɛlamnaa) |
| أنْتُمْ | دَرَّسْتُمْ | (darrastum) | سابَقْتُمْ | (saabaqtum) | أَعْلَمْتُمْ | ('aɛlamtum) |
| أنْتُنَّ | دَرَّسْتُنَّ | (darrastunna) | سابَقْتُنَّ | (saabaqtunna) | أَعْلَمْتُنَّ | ('aɛlamtunna) |
| هُم | دَرَّسوا | (darrasuu) | سابَقوا | (saabaquu) | أَعْلَموا | ('aɛlamuu) |
| هُنَّ | دَرَّسْنَ | (darrasna) | سابَقْنَ | (saabaqna) | أَعْلَمْنَ | ('aɛlamna) |

## Present

| | Form II (*yufaععil*) | Form III (*yufaaعil*) | Form IV (*yufعil*) | |
|---|---|---|---|---|
| *singular* | | | | |
| أَنَا | أُدَرِّس ('udarris[u]) | أُسَابِق ('usaabiq[u]) | أُعْلِم ('uعlim[u]) | |
| أَنْتَ | تُدَرِّس (tudarris[u]) | تُسَابِق (tusaabiq[u]) | تُعْلِم (tuعlim[u]) | |
| أَنْتِ | تُدَرِّسِينَ (tudarrisiina) | تُسَابِقِينَ (tusaabiqiina) | تُعْلِمِينَ (tuعlimiina) | |
| هُوَ | يُدَرِّس (yudarris[u]) | يُسَابِق (yusaabiq[u]) | يُعْلِم (yuعlim[u]) | |
| هِيَ | تُدَرِّس (tudarris[u]) | تُسَابِق (tusaabiq[u]) | تُعْلِم (tuعlim[u]) | |

*plural*

| | Form II | Form III | Form IV | |
|---|---|---|---|---|
| نَحْنُ | نُدَرِّس (nudarris[u]) | نُسَابِق (nusaabiq[u]) | نُعْلِم (nuعlim[u]) | |
| أَنْتُمْ | تُدَرِّسُونَ (tudarrisuuna) | تُسَابِقُونَ (tusaabiquuna) | تُعْلِمُونَ (tuعlimuuna) | |
| أَنْتُنَّ | تُدَرِّسْنَ (tudarrisna) | تُسَابِقْنَ (tusaabiqna) | تُعْلِمْنَ (tuعlimna) | |
| هُم | يُدَرِّسُونَ (yudarrisuuna) | يُسَابِقُونَ (yusaabiquuna) | يُعْلِمُونَ (yuعlimuuna) | |
| هُنَّ | يُدَرِّسْنَ (yudarrisna) | يُسَابِقْنَ (yusaabiqna) | يُعْلِمْنَ (yuعlimna) | |

صَيْد السَّمَك يُعَلِّم الصَّبْر.

Fishing [*lit*: hunting fish] teaches patience.

سَنُحاوِل اليَوْم أَن نَذْهَب إِلَى النَّهر.

We will try to go to the river today.

الشَّمْس القَوِّية سَخَّنَت الماء.

The hot [*lit:* strong] sun has warmed the water.

العُمّال أَخْرَجوا الزَّبالة.

The workers have removed the garbage.

مَنْ سَيُدَرِّس لَنا اللُّغة اليابانِيَّة؟

Who's going to teach us Japanese [*lit*: the Japanese language]?

# Irregular verbs in forms II–IV

Verbs that are irregular in the basic form often also show irregularities in the derived forms. You should still try to apply the same basic rules for the different types of irregular verb: weak verbs, doubled verbs, and verbs with *hamza* as a root letter (see Chapters 4–6). Note that, in general, if a form requires doubling a root letter or separating root letters with a long vowel, then a basic verb with a doubled or weak root letter (*waaw* or *yaa'*) will often behave perfectly regularly when put into these patterns. Here are some notes about how irregular verbs behave in forms II–IV, followed by a summary table:

**Doubled verbs:**
• Doubled verbs behave as *regular* verbs in form II. (Doubling the middle root letter means that the second and third root letters of a doubled verb are always written separately.)
• Doubled verbs in forms III and IV follow the same rules as for the basic doubled verb (see page 30). Form IV doubled verbs are much more common than form III.

**Verbs with *hamza* as a root letter:**
• Verbs with *hamza* behave roughly as *regular* verbs, but see rules about spelling on page 30. Note in particular the rule about writing two *hamzas* carried by *'alif* together as a *madda* ( آ ). This rule means the past tense of forms III and IV starts with this combination when *hamza* is the first root letter (see table).
• When *hamza* is the middle (second) root letter, you may see it by itself on the line in form III because it follows a long vowel (see page 34).

**Weak verbs:**
• Verbs with *waaw* or *yaa'* as the first or second root letter (*assimilated* and *hollow* verbs) behave as *regular* verbs in forms II and III.
• *Assimilated* verbs in form IV have a long *uu* vowel at the beginning of the present tense (see table).
• *Hollow* verbs in form IV behave like basic verbs. They have a short vowel in the middle if the third root letter has a *sukuun* over it, but this is the short vowel connected to the <u>derived</u> pattern and not to the

original root. For example, "I wanted" = أَرَدْتُ (*'aradtu*). The short vowel is a *fatHa* because the form IV past pattern is أَفْعَلَ (*'afala*). Verbs with *waaw* or *yaa'* as the third root (*defective*) behave irregularly in all forms. Forms II, III and IV *defective* verbs all have the same endings as the يمشي/مشى basic group of verbs (see pages 27–28).

|  | **Form II**<br>(*yufaɛɛil*) | | **Form III**<br>(*yufaaɛil*) | | **Form IV**<br>(*yufɛil*) | |
|---|---|---|---|---|---|---|
| **Doubled verbs** | | | | | | |
| past | رَدَّدَ | repeated | ضَادَّ | opposed | أَحَبَّ | liked |
| present | يُرَدِّد | repeats | يُضَادّ | opposes | يُحِبّ | likes |
| **Verbs with hamza** | | | | | | |
| *as 1st root letter:* | | | | | | |
| past | أَثَّرَ | influenced | آخَذَ | blamed | آمَنَ | believed (in) |
| present | يُؤَثِّر | influences | يُوَاخِذ | blames | يُؤْمِن | believes (in) |
| *as 2nd root letter:* | | | | | | |
| past | *no verbs in* | | سَاءَلَ | questioned | أَسْأَمَ | bored |
| present | *common circulation* | | يُسَائِل | questions | يُسْئِم | bores |
| *as 3nd root letter:* | | | | | | |
| past | هَنَّأَ | congratulated | كَافَأَ | rewarded | أَنْشَأَ | founded |
| present | يُهَنِّئ | congratulates | يكَافِئ | rewards | يُنْشِئ | founds |
| **Weak verbs** | | | | | | |
| *assimilated (1st root):* | | | | | | |
| past | يَسَّرَ | facilitated | وَافَقَ | agreed with | أَوْصَلَ | connected |
| present | يُيَسِّر | facilitates | يُوَافِق | agrees with | يُوصِل | connects |
| *hollow (2nd root):* | | | | | | |
| past | خَوَّفَ | frightened | نَاوَلَ | handed over | أَرَادَ | wanted |
| present | يُخَوِّف | frightens | يُنَاوِل | hands over | يُرِيد | wants |
| *defective (3rd root):* | | | | | | |
| past | رَبَّى | bred/raised | لاقَى | met with | أَعْطَى | gave |
| present | يُرَبِّي | breeds/raises | يُلاقِي | meets with | يُعطِي | gives |

# Summary of forms II–IV

- Form II verbs are characterized by the doubling of the second root letter (يُفَعِّل – *yufaξξil*).

- Form III verbs are characterized by the long *aa* vowel after the first root letter (يُفاعِل – *yufaaξil*).

- Form IV verbs are characterized by the *sukuun* over the first root letter (يُفْعِل – *yufξil*).

- Forms II–IV are the only Arabic verbs to have a *Damma* as the first vowel in the present tense (*yudarris, nuHaawil*, etc.)

- Forms II and IV are most often used with a *transitive* or *causative* meaning (doing something <u>to</u> something/someone else). Form III is most often used for mutual actions (doing something <u>with</u> someone else). However, there are also many other possible meaning patterns.

- Verbs that are irregular in the basic form may also act irregularly in the derived forms (see table on page 41).

# 9 Derived forms V–VI

The second of the groups of derived forms is made up of forms V (يَتَفَعَّل – *yatafaεεal*) and VI (يَتَفاعَل – *yatafaaεal*).

## Characteristics

**Past tense**

- Form V is made by adding تَ (*ta*) on the front of the form II pattern:
فَعَّل (form II *faεεala*) ➔ تَفَعَّل (form V verb *tafaεεala*)

- Form VI is made by adding تَ (*ta*) on the front of the form III pattern
فَاعَل (form III *faaεala*) ➔ تَفَاعَل (form VI verb *tafaaεala*)

**Present tense**

In the present tense, these two forms are vowelized throughout with *fatHa* (ﹷ):

Form V: يَتَفَعَّل (*yatafaεεal*)
Form VI: يَتَفاعَل (*yatafaaεal*)

## Common meaning patterns

**1.** Form V can be connected to form II in meaning as well as structure. Form V is often the *reflexive* of form II. In other words, it has the meaning of performing an action <u>on yourself</u>:

يُذَكِّر (form II verb *yudhakkir* – to remind)➔
يَتَذَكَّر (form V verb *yatadhakkar* – to remember ["remind yourself"])

Notice that this can mean some form V verbs are very close in meaning to the original basic root verb and can even sometimes be alternatives with almost the <u>same</u> meaning:

يَعْلِم (basic verb *yaҁ lam* – to know)→

يُعَلِّم (form II verb *yuҁ allim* – to instruct)→

يَتَعَلَّم (form V verb *yataҁ allam* – to learn)

**2.** As form V is often the reflexive of form II, so form VI is <u>sometimes</u> the reflexive of form III, producing the meaning of doing something together or as a group:

يُعاوِن (form III verb *yuҁ aawin* – to help)→

يَتَعَاوَن (form IV verb *yataҁ aawan* – to cooperate ["to help each other"])

يُحادِث (form III verb *yuHaadith* – to talk to someone)→

يَتَحادَث (form VI verb *yataHaadath* – to converse/talk together

**3.** Some form VI verbs are connected with a state, where in English we might use an adjective ("to be lazy," "to be annoyed," etc.). You should also be aware that there are also many form V and VI verbs that have no particular logic (or the logic is lost in the history of the language!): Here is a table showing the past and present tenses of forms V and VI,

يَتَكاسَل (*yatakaasal)* – to be lazy

يَتَضايَق (*yataDaayaq)* – to be annoyed

يَتَوَقَّف (*yatawaqqaf)*– to stop

يَتَصَرَّف (*yataSarraf)* – to behave

followed by some example sentences:

## Past

| singular | Form V<br>*(tafaɛɛala)* | | Form VI<br>*(tafaaɛala)* | |
|---|---|---|---|---|
| أنا | تَذَكَّرْتُ | (tadhakkartu) | تَحادَثْتُ | (taHaadathtu) |
| أنْتَ | تَذَكَّرْتَ | (tadhakkarta) | تَحادَثْتَ | (taHaadathta) |
| أنْتِ | تَذَكَّرْتِ | (tadhakkarti) | تَحادَثْتِ | (taHaadathti) |
| هُوَ | تَذَكَّرَ | (tadhakkara) | تَحادَثَ | (taHaadatha) |
| هِيَ | تَذَكَّرَتْ | (tadhakkarat) | تَحادَثَتْ | (taHaadathat) |

*plural*

| | Form V | | Form VI | |
|---|---|---|---|---|
| نَحْنُ | تَذَكَّرْنا | (tadhakkarnaa) | تَحادَثْنا | (taHaadathnaa) |
| أنْتُمْ | تَذَكَّرْتُمْ | (tadhakkartum) | تَحادَثْتُمْ | (taHaadathtum) |
| أنْتُنَّ | تَذَكَّرْتُنَّ | (tadhakkartunna) | تَحادَثْتُنَّ | (taHaadathtunna) |
| هُم | تَذَكَّروا | (tadhakkaruu) | تَحادَثوا | (taHaadathuu) |
| هُنَّ | تَذَكَّرْنَ | (tadhakkarna) | تَحادَثْنَ | (taHaadathna) |

## Present

| | Form V<br>(*yatafaεεal*) | | Form VI<br>(*yatafaaεal*) |
|---|---|---|---|
| *singular* | | | |
| أنا | أَتَذَكَّر ('atadhakkar[u]) | أَتَحَادَث | ('ataHaadith[u]) |
| أنْتَ | تَتَذَكَّر (tatadhakkar[u]) | تَتَحَادَث | (tataHaadith[u]) |
| أنْتِ | تَتَذَكَّرينَ (tatadhakkariina) | تَتَحَادَثينَ | (tataHaadithiina) |
| هُوَ | يَتَذَكَّر (yatadhakkar[u]) | يَتَحَادَث | (yataHaadith[u]) |
| هِيَ | تَتَذَكَّر (tatadhakkar[u]) | تَتَحَادَث | (tataHaadith[u]) |

*plural*

| | | | |
|---|---|---|---|
| نَحْنُ | نَتَذَكَّر (natadhakkar[u]) | نَتَحَادَث | (nataHaadith[u]) |
| أنْتُمْ | تَتَذَكَّرونَ (tatadhakkaruuna) | تَتَحَادَثونَ | (tataHaadithuuna) |
| أنتُن | تَتَذَكَّرْنَ (tatadhakkarna) | تَتَحَادَثْنَ | (tataHaadithna) |
| هُم | يَتَذَكَّرونَ (yatadhakkaruuna) | يَتَحَادَثونَ | (yataHaadithuuna) |
| هُنَّ | يَتَذَكَّرْنَ (yatadhakkarna) | يَتَحَادَثْنَ | (yataHaadithna) |

أَنَا لا أَتَذَكَّر اسْمَكَ.

I don't remember your name.

تَكَاسَلْتُ في الصَّباح فَفاتَني القِطار.

I was lazy in the morning, and so I missed the train.

بَعْض النَّاس يَتَصَرَّفونَ بِطَريقة غَريبة.

Some people behave in a strange manner.

تَعَطَّرَت الفَتاة قَبْلَ خُروجِها.

The girl put on perfume before she went out [lit: before her exit].

هَلْ تَتَضَايَق مِن الدُّخَان؟

Does the smoke bother you?

# Irregular verbs in forms V and VI

Because of the close link between forms V–VI and II–III, you will find that many of the same rules apply to the irregular verbs in both cases.

**Doubled verbs:**
• Doubled verbs behave as regular verbs in form V (as for form II, doubling the middle root letter means that the second and third root letters of a doubled verb are always written separately.)
• Doubled verbs in form VI will follow the same rules as for the basic doubled verb (see page 30) but are rare and not worth too much attention.

**Verbs with *hamza* as a root letter:**
• Verbs with *hamza* behave roughly as regular verbs, but see rules about spelling on page 34. Because past and present verbs in forms V and VI are nearly always vowelized with *fatHas* (‗), you will usually see the *hamza* written on an *'alif* (أ).
• When *hamza* is the middle (second) root letter, it can be written by itself on the line in form VI (as in form III) because it follows a long vowel (see page 30).

**Weak verbs:**
• Verbs with *waaw* or *yaa'* as the first or second root letter (*assimilated* and *hollow* verbs) behave as *regular* verbs in forms V and VI, as they do in forms II and III.
• Verbs with *waaw* or *yaa'* as the third root (*defective*) behave irregularly in both forms. *Defective* verbs in forms V and VI are characterized by an *'alif maqsuura* at the end of both the past and present tenses — *aa* vowel written on a *yaa'* without dots, see Appendix (i). This is the same ending as the مشى basic group of verbs in the past tense, but like the ينسى group in the present tense (see pages 27–28).

|  | **Form V**<br>(*yatafaɛɛal*) | | **Form VI**<br>(*yatafaaɛal*) | |
|---|---|---|---|---|
| **Doubled verbs** | | | | |
| past | تَرَدَّدَ | hesitated | *no verbs in* | |
| present | يَتَرَدَّد | hesitates | *common circulation* | |
| **Verbs with hamza** | | | | |
| *as 1st root letter:* | | | | |
| past | تَأَثَّرَ | was influenced | تَآلَفَ | were familiar |
| present | يَتَأَثَّر | is influenced | يَتَآلَف | are familiar |
| *as 2nd root letter:* | | | | |
| past | تَفَأَّلَ | boded well of | تَسَاءَلَ | wondered |
| present | يَتَفَأَّل | bodes well of | يَتَسَاءَل | wonders |
| *as 3nd root letter:* | | | | |
| past | تَنَبَّأَ | predicted | تَكَافَأَ | were equal |
| present | يَتَنَبَّأَ | predicts | يَتَكَافَأَ | are equal |
| **Weak verbs** | | | | |
| *assimilated (1st root):* | | | | |
| past | تَوَقَّعَ | expected | تَوَافَقَ | agreed together |
| present | يَتَوَقَّع | expects | يَتَوَافَق | agree together |
| *hollow (2nd root):* | | | | |
| past | تَلَوَّنَ | was colored (in) | تَعَاوَنَ | cooperated |
| present | يَتَلَوَّن | is colored (in) | يَتَعَاوَن | cooperate |
| *defective (3rd root):* | | | | |
| past | تَمَنَّى | wished/wanted | تَلاقَى | met together |
| present | يَتَمَنَّى | wishes/wants | يَتَلاقَى | meet together |

# Summary of forms V–VI

- Form V and VI verbs are characterized by the ‏تَ‎ (*ta*) in front of the root letters.

- Form V verbs also double the middle root letter, like form II (‏يَتَفَعَّل‎ – *yatafaᵹᵹal*).

- Form VI verbs also add a long *aa* after the first root letter, like form III (‏يَتَفاعَل‎ – *yatafaaᵹal*).

- Form V and VI verbs are vowelized throughout with *fatHa* (‏ـَ‎) in the past and present tenses.

- Forms V and VI can be the *passive* of forms II and III. Form VI often carries the meaning of "doing something together in a group."

- Verbs that are irregular in the basic form may also act irregularly in these derived forms (see table page 52).

# 10 Derived forms VII–X

The third group of derived forms is made of up forms VII (يَنْفَعِل –
*yanfaɛil*), VIII (يَفْتَعِل – *yaftaɛil*), and X (يَسْتَفْعِل – *yastafɛil*). Form IX
(characterized by doubling the final root letter) has virtually died out in
modern Arabic. The only context in which you might see it is
connected with changing color, e.g.: يَحْمَرّ (*yaHmarr*) – "turn red" or
"blush," etc.

## Characteristics

**Past tense**

- Form VII is made by adding *in* (اِنْ) in front of the root letters:

  فَعَلَ (basic verb *faɛala*)  ➔  اِنْفَعَلَ (form VII verb *infaɛala*)

- Form VIII is made by adding *i* (اِ) in front of the first root letter and
  *taa'* (ت) after it:

  فَعَلَ (basic verb *faɛala*)  ➔  اِفْتَعَلَ (form VIII verb *iftaɛala*)

- Form X is formed by adding an *ista* (اِسْتَ) in front of the root letters
  and putting a *sukuun* over the first root letter:

  فَعَلَ (basic verb *faɛala*)  ➔  اِسْتَفْعَلَ (form VIII verb *istafɛala*)

**Present tense**

In the present tense, these three forms keep the same basic features of
the past tense but are vowelized differently. They all have a *fatHa* (َ) as
the first two vowels and a *kasra* (ِ) as the third:

Form VII: يَنْفَعِل (*yanfaɛil*)

Form VIII: يَفْتَعِل (*yaftaɛil*)

Form X: يَسْتَفْعِل (*yastafɛil*)

## Other characteristics

• The *kasra* (*i*) that begins the past tense of all these three forms will disappear (elide) if the word before <u>ends</u> with a vowel. This is because the *kasra* is carried by *hamzat al waSl* – see Appendix (i).

اِنْقَلَبَ مَرْكِبُهُ. (*inqalaba markibuhu*) – His boat turned over.

but

ثُمَّ انْقَلَبَ مَرْكِبُهُ. (*thumma nqalaba markibuhu*) – Then his boat turned over.

• Form VII is almost never formed with verbs whose first root letter is *hamza* (ء), *waaw* (و), *yaa'* (ي), *nuun* (ن), *lam* (ل), or *ra'* (ر). The combination of sounds would be unnatural in Arabic.

• The first root letter can affect the beginning of Form VIII verbs. These can seem complicated but follow these general rules:

– When the first root letter is *ta'* (ت), *waaw* (و) or *hamza* (ء), this is replaced by a doubling of the *ta'* at the beginning of the pattern:

يَتَّخِذِ/اِتَّخَذَ (*yattakhidh/ittakhadha*: "to adopt") – from the root: أخذ

يَتَّفِق/اِتَّفَقَ (*yattafiq/ittafaqa*: "to agree") – from the root: وفق

– When the first root letter is *daal* (د), *dhaal* (ذ) or *zaay* (ز), the *ta'* at the beginning of form VIII is replaced by a *daal*. In the case of *daal* and *dhaal,* this is then usually combined with the first root letter to produce a double *daal*:

يَزْدَحِم/اِزْدَحَمَ (*yazdaHim/izdaHama*: "to crowd") – from the root: زحم

يَدَّخِر/اِدَّخَرَ (*yaddakhkhir/iddakhkhara*: "to store") – from the root: ذخر

– When the first root letter is *Taa'* (ط), *Zaa'* (ظ), *Saad* (ص) or *Daad* (ض), the *ta'* at the beginning of form VIII is replaced by a *Taa'*. In the case of *Taa'* and *Zaa',* this is then usually combined with the first root letter to produce a double *Taa'*:

يَضْطَرِب/إضْطَرَبَ (yaDTarib/iDTaraba: "to be disturbed") – from
the root: ضرب

يَطَّلِع/إطَّلَعَ (yaTTaliε/iTTalaεa: "to know about") – from the root: طلع

# Common meaning patterns

**1.** Form VII is relatively uncommon and usually has a passive
meaning:

يَقْلِب (basic verb *yaqlib* – to overturn/turn [something] over)➤

يَنْقَلِب (form VII verb *yanqalib* – to be overturned)

يَكْسَر (basic verb *yaksar* – to break)➤

يَنْكَسِر (form VII verb *yankasir* – to be broken)

**2.** Form VIII is a common form and is usually intransitive, but there is
no consistent meaning pattern connected with it. These verbs are often
close to the basic root meaning:

يَجْمَع (basic verb *yajmaε* – to gather/put together)➤

يَجْتَمِع (form VIII verb *yajtamiε* – to assemble/meet together)

يَقْرُب (basic verb *yaqrub* – to be near)➤

يَقْتَرِب (form VIII verb *yaqtarib* – to approach/advance)

يَنْشُر (basic verb *yanshur* – to publish/diffuse)➤

يَنْتَشِر (form VIII verb *yaqtarib* – to become widespread)

**3.** Form X often has the meaning of <u>asking</u> for something:

يَأْذَن (basic verb *ya'dhan* – to permit)➤

يَسْتَأْذِن (form X verb *yasta'dhin* – to ask for permission)

يَعْلَم (basic verb *yaεlam* – to know)➤

يَسْتَعْلِم (form X verb *yastaεlim* – to inquire ["ask for knowledge"])

**4.** Form X can also mean to "consider or find something ...":

يَحْسُن (basic verb *yaHsun* – to be beautiful)➡

يَسْتَحْسِن (form X verb *yastaHsin* – to admire ["consider beautiful"])

Here is a table showing the past and present tenses for these three verb forms, followed by some example sentences:

## Past

|  | | Form VII<br>(*infaɛala*) | | Form VIII<br>(*iftaɛala*) | | Form X<br>(*istafɛala*) |
| --- | --- | --- | --- | --- | --- | --- |
| *singular* | | | | | | |
| أَنا | اِنْقَلَبْتُ | (inqalabtu) | اِقْتَرَبْتُ | (iqtatabtu) | اِسْتَعْلَمْتُ | (istaɛlamtu) |
| أَنْتَ | اِنْقَلَبْتَ | (inqalabta) | اِقْتَرَبْتَ | (iqtatabta) | اِسْتَعْلَمْتَ | (istaɛlamta) |
| أَنْتِ | اِنْقَلَبْتِ | (inqalabti) | اِقْتَرَبْتِ | (iqtatabti) | اِسْتَعْلَمْتِ | (istaɛlamti) |
| هُوَ | اِنْقَلَبَ | (inqalaba) | اِقْتَرَبَ | (iqtataba) | اِسْتَعْلَمَ | (istaɛlama) |
| هِيَ | اِنْقَلَبَتْ | (inqalabat) | اِقْتَرَبَتْ | (iqtatabat) | اِسْتَعْلَمَتْ | (istaɛlamat) |
| *plural* | | | | | | |
| نَحْنُ | اِنْقَلَبْنا | (inqalabnaa) | اِقْتَرَبْنا | (iqtatabnaa) | اِسْتَعْلَمْنا | (istaɛlamnaa) |
| أَنْتُمْ | اِنْقَلَبْتُمْ | (inqalabtum) | اِقْتَرَبْتُمْ | (iqtatabtum) | اِسْتَعْلَمْتُمْ | (istaɛlamtum) |
| أَنْتُنَّ | اِنْقَلَبْتُنَّ | (inqalabtunna) | اِقْتَرَبْتُنَّ | (iqtatabtunna) | اِسْتَعْلَمْتُنَّ | (istaɛlamtunna) |
| هُم | اِنْقَلَبُوا | (inqalabuu) | اِقْتَرَبُوا | (iqtatabuu) | اِسْتَعْلَمُوا | (istaɛlamuu) |
| هُنَّ | اِنْقَلَبْنَ | (inqalabna) | اِقْتَرَبْنَ | (iqtatabna) | اِسْتَعْلَمْنَ | (istaɛlamna) |

## Present

| singular | Form VII<br>(yanfaɛil) | | Form VIII<br>(yaftaɛil) | | Form X<br>(yastafɛil) | |
|---|---|---|---|---|---|---|
| أنا | أَنْقَلِب | ('anqalib[u]) | أَقْتَرِب | ('aqtarib[u]) | أَسْتَعْلِم | ('astaɛlim[u]) |
| أَنْتَ | تَنْقَلِب | (tanqalib[u]) | تَقْتَرِب | (taqtarib[u]) | تَسْتَعْلِم | (tastaɛlim[u]) |
| أَنْتِ | تَنْقَلِبِينَ | (tanqalibiina) | تَقْتَرِبِينَ | (taqtaribiina) | تَسْتَعْلِمِينَ | (tastaɛlimiina) |
| هُوَ | يَنْقَلِب | (yanqalib[u]) | يَقْتَرِب | (yaqtarib[u]) | يَسْتَعْلِم | (yastaɛlim[u]) |
| هِيَ | تَنْقَلِب | (tanqalib[u]) | تَقْتَرِب | (taqtarib[u]) | تَسْتَعْلِم | (tastaɛlim[u]) |

*plural*

| | Form VII | | Form VIII | | Form X | |
|---|---|---|---|---|---|---|
| نَحْنُ | نَنْقَلِب | (nanqalib[u]) | نَقْتَرِب | (naqtarib[u]) | نَسْتَعْلِم | (nastaɛlim[u]) |
| أَنْتُمْ | تَنْقَلِبُونَ | (tanqalibuuna) | تَقْتَرِبُونَ | (taqtaribuuna) | تَسْتَعْلِمُونَ | (tastaɛlimuuna) |
| أَنْتُنَّ | تَنْقَلِبْنَ | (tanqalibna) | تَقْتَرِبْنَ | (taqtaribna) | تَسْتَعْلِمْنَ | (tastaɛlimna) |
| هُم | يَنْقَلِبُونَ | (yanqalibuuna) | يَقْتَرِبُونَ | (yaqtaribuuna) | يَسْتَعْلِمُونَ | (yastaɛlimuuna) |
| هُنَّ | يَنْقَلِبْنَ | (yanqalibna) | يَقْتَرِبْنَ | (yaqtaribna) | يَسْتَعْلِمْنَ | (yastaɛlimna) |

إِنْقَلَبَت السَفِينة في العاصِفة.

The ship capsized in the storm.

شَعَرْنا بالحَرارة حَيْنَ اقْتَرَبْنا مِن الفُرْن.

We felt the heat when we approached the oven.

يَسْتَعْلِم السائِح من الدَليل عَنْ مكان الأهْرام.

The tourist ask the guide about the location of the pyramids.

إِنْقَسَمَت البيتْزا إلى أرْبَعة أجْزاء.

The pizza was divided into four pieces.

إسْتَخْرَجَ الجَرّاح الرَّصاصة مِن كِتْفي.

The surgeon removed the bullet from my shoulder.

# Irregular verbs in forms VII–X

Here are some notes about how irregular verbs behave in forms VII–X, followed by a summary table:

**Doubled verbs:**
• Doubled verbs in forms VII, VIII, and X follow the same rules as for the basic doubled verb (see page 30).

**Verbs with *hamza* as a root letter:**
• Verbs with *hamza* are not common in forms VII–X. When they do occur, they behave roughly as *regular* verbs, but see rules about spelling on page 34. Note in particular that form VIII verbs with *hamza* as the first letter behave like assimilated verbs (see table).

**Weak verbs:**
• *Assimilated* verbs are virtually nonexistent in form VII and regular in form X. In form VIII, the first letter drops out and is replaced by a doubling of the *taa'*.
• *Hollow* verbs in forms VII–X behave similarly to basic hollow verbs. They have a long vowel at the end if there is no *sukuun* over the third root letter. Notice that this long vowel is usually an *aa* sound ( ـا ). Only in the present tense of form X is it an *ii* sound ( ـِ ). If the third root letter has a *sukuun* over it, the long vowel will become short. For example, "he resigned" = اِسْتَقَال (*istaqaala*), but "I resigned" = اِسْتَقَلْتُ (*istaqaltu*).
• Verbs with *waaw* or *yaa'* as the third root (*defective*) behave irregularly in forms VII, VIII, and X and have the same endings as the يمشي/مشى basic group of verbs (see pages 27–28).

|  | **Form VII** <br> *(yanfaε il)* | | **Form VIII** <br> *(yaftaε il)* | | **Form X** <br> *(yastafε il)* | |
|---|---|---|---|---|---|---|
| **Doubled verbs** | | | | | | |
| past | اِنْضَمَّ | joined (club) | اِمْتَدّ | extended | اِسْتَمَرّ | continued |
| present | يَنْضَمّ | joins (club) | يَمْتَدّ | extend | يَسْتَمِرّ | continues |
| **Verbs with hamza** | | | | | | |
| *as 1st root letter:* | | | | | | |
| past | *no verbs in* | | اِتَّخَذَ | adopted | اِسْتَأْجَرَ | rented |
| present | *common circulation* | | يَتَّخِذ | adopt | يَسْتَأْجِر | rents |
| *as 2nd root letter:* | | | | | | |
| past | *no verbs in* | | اِبْتَأَسَ | was sad | *no verbs in* | |
| present | *common circulation* | | يَبْتَئِس | is sad | *common circulation* | |
| *as 3rd root letter:* | | | | | | |
| past | اِنْقَرَأَ | was read | اِبْتَدَأَ | began | اِسْتَمْرَأَ | savored |
| present | يَنْقَرِئ | is read | يَبْتَدِئ | begins | يَسْتَمْرِئ | savors |
| **Weak verbs** | | | | | | |
| *assimilated (1st root):* | | | | | | |
| past | *no verbs in* | | اِتَّفَقَ | agreed | اِسْتَوْقَفَ | stopped |
| present | *common circulation* | | يَتَّفِق | agrees | يَسْتَوْقِف | stops |
| *hollow (2nd root):* | | | | | | |
| past | اِنْقَادَ | was led | اِحْتَاجَ | needed | اِسْتَقَالَ | resigned |
| present | يَنْقَاد | is led | يَحْتَاج | needs | يَستقيل | resigns |
| *defective (3rd root):* | | | | | | |
| past | اِنْحَنَى | was bent | اِشْتَرَى | bought | اِسْتَثْنَى | excluded |
| present | يَنْحَنِي | is bent | يَشْتَرِي | buys | يَسْتَثْنِي | excludes |

# Summary of forms VII-X

- Form VII verbs are characterized by the *nuun* (ن) before the root letters (يَنْفَعِل – *yanfaɛil*).

- Form VIII verbs are characterized by the *taa'* (ت) after the first root letter (يَفْتَعِل – *yaftaɛil*). This form can change somewhat depending on the first root letter.

- Form X verbs are characterized by the *siin* (س) and *taa'* (ت) – or *sta* sound – before the root letters (يَسْتَفْعِل – *yastafɛil*).

- In the past tense, forms VII–X start with i (١): *infaɛala, iftaɛala, istafɛala.*

- In the present tense, forms VII–X are vowelled with 2 *fatHas* and a *kasra*: *yanfaɛil, yaftaɛil, yastafɛil.*

- Form VII often has a *passive* meaning (to have something done to you).

- Form VIII is a common form but has no consistent meaning patterns associated with it.

- Form X has two common meaning patterns: to think or consider that something is (beautiful, etc.), and to ask for something.

# 11 Essentials of making sentences with verbs

The first chapters of this book have covered the essentials of Arabic verbs — the basic tenses and forms. Before we move on to look at some of the more detailed aspects of how verbs are used, we need to recap and expand on how to use verbs in sentences.

Some information on how verbs behave in sentences has already been presented in the first ten verb chapters. Below is a summary of this information with important additional notes.

- Arabic verbs change according to the *subject* (who/what is carrying out the action):

  كَتَبَ خالِد رِسالة لِلوَزير. Khalid wrote (*kataba*) a letter to the minister.

  كَتَبَتْ فاطمة رِسالة لِلوَزير. Fatma wrote (*katabat*) a letter to the minister.

- If the subject is a mixed group of male and female people, the masculine is used:

  الأوْلاد والبَنات دَخَلُوا المَدْرَسة. The boys and girls entered the school.

  [There are different endings/beginnings for two people or things (the Dual). These are covered in Chapter 18 (for verbs) and Chapter 28 (in general).]

- Because the *prefixes* and *suffixes* (letters on the beginning and end of the verb) tell you the subject, Arabic does not often use personal pronouns with verbs (e.g., أنا – "I," هُوَ – "he," etc.). If they are used, it is usually for emphasis and comes after the verb:

  دَخَلَ أخي جامِعة القاهِرة في عام ١٩٩٥، ثُمَّ بَعدَ سَنتَيْن دَخَلْتُ أنا.
  My brother attended Cairo University in 1995, then two years later I [too] attended.

- The verb can come before or after the subject. This is largely a matter of emphasis/level of formality. If a sentence starts with the subject, you might see the word إِنَّ (*'inna*) first. This word is added for emphasis but has no direct translation:

كَتَبَ خالِدٌ رسالةً لِلوَزير. (verb before subject)

إِنَّ خالِدًا كَتَبَ رسالةً لِلوَزير. (subject before verb with إِنَّ)

إِنَّ is followed by the accusative case (خالِدًا – *khaalidan*) – see Appendix (ii).

- The plural verbs are only used for people. If the subject of a verb is plural but <u>not human</u> (i.e., three or more things/ideas, etc.), Arabic grammar regards this as <u>feminine singular</u> (refer to Chapter 21 if you need to review this concept). This means you have to use the هِيَ ("she") part of the verb:

وقَعَت الصُحُون عَلَى الأَرْض وانْكَسَرَت. The plates fell on the floor and broke.

إِنَّ الدُوَل الإِسْلاميَّة تَتَعاوَن مِنْ أَجْل السلام. The Islamic states are cooperating for [the sake of] peace.

This is a very important aspect of Arabic grammar generally since there is virtually no exception to the rule. It might seem odd to you to refer to a group of plates or countries as "she", but it will seem just as odd to an Arabic speaker if you use the plural forms which they reserve for people!

- If the subject is a group of people, the verb will still be singular if it comes <u>before</u> the subject. It will only change according to whether the subject is masculine or feminine:

وصَل الرجال إِلَى المَصْنَع. The men arrived at the factory.

بَدَأَت السَيِّدات اجْتِماعهُنَّ. The women began their meeting.

Look at the next sentences. They have two verbs, before and after the subject:

حَضَرَ المُدَرِّسون اجْتِماعاً واتَّفَقُوا عَلَى البَرْنامِج لِلعام القادِم.
The teachers attended a meeting and agreed on the program for the upcoming year.

كَتَبَت البَنات خِطابات، ثُمَّ خَرَجْنَ.
The girls wrote letters and then went out.

The subject of the first sentence above is <u>masculine plural</u> (*mudarrisuuna* – teachers). The first verb (*HaDara* – attended) has the masculine singular ending *a* because it comes before the subject. The second verb (*ittafaquu* – agreed) has the plural ending *uu* since it comes after the subject. The same is true of the second sentence, except that the subject is now <u>feminine plural</u> (*banaat* – girls) and so the feminine singular ending *at* (*katabat* – wrote) and feminine plural ending *na* (*kharajna* – went out) are used.

These are the basic guidelines for using verbs. You will become more aware of subtle style differences through reading and absorbing Arabic that is written in a natural style by native speakers.

# 12 Verbs in the subjunctive

In previous chapters, we have seen how different verbs work in the standard present tense. Now we need to look at some variations that can occur to the present verb in certain situations. Grammarians often call these variations "moods of the verb." The two moods you need to know in Arabic are the *subjunctive* and the *jussive*. Only in the minority of cases do these moods affect the way a verb is written or pronounced. However, you do need to know the whole story, otherwise you cannot understand or work out the changes that occur in this significant minority of cases.

The individual usages of the subjunctive and jussive listed in the next two chapters are relatively limited and easy to remember. You will soon come to connect them with particular words and phrases.

## Regular verbs in the subjunctive

In regular verbs, the subjunctive is very similar to the standard present tense. This is also true of the derived forms.

The most significant change is that when the standard present tense ends in a *nuun* (ن), this is dropped in the *subjunctive*. This affects the masculine plurals – هُم (*hum*) and أَنْتُم (*'antum*) – and the feminine أَنْتِ (*'anti*) parts of the verb. (The dual is also affected – see Chapter 28). These changes affect the script and pronunciation.

Less significantly, the unpronounced *Damma* (◌ُ) that ends many parts of the standard present tense (see page 15) changes to a *fatHa* (◌َ) in the subjunctive. In other words يَكْتُبُ (*yaktubu*) becomes يَكْتُبَ (*yaktuba*).

As both these alternatives are usually written without vowels and pronounced يَكْتُب (*yaktub*), you would not normally notice the change.

The table below shows the standard present tense and the subjunctive for the regular verb *yaktub* (to write):

|  | | **Standard present** | **Subjunctive** |
|---|---|---|---|
| *singular* | | | |
| أنا I | | أَكْتُبُ 'aktub(u) | أَكْتُبَ 'aktub(a) |
| أنْتَ you (masc.) | | تَكْتُبُ taktub(u) | تَكْتُبَ taktub(a) |
| أنْتِ you (fem.) | | تَكْتُبِينَ taktubiina | تَكْتُبِي taktubii |
| هُوَ he/it | | يَكْتُبُ yaktub(u) | يَكْتُبَ yaktub(a) |
| هِيَ she/it | | تَكْتُبُ taktub(u) | تَكْتُبَ taktub(a) |
| *plural* | | | |
| نَحْنُ we | | نَكْتُبُ naktub(u) | نَكْتُبَ naktub(a) |
| أنْتُمْ you (masc. pl) | | تَكْتُبُونَ taktubuuna | تَكْتُبُوا* taktubuu |
| أنْتُنَّ you (fem. pl) | | تَكْتُبْنَ taktubna | تَكْتُبْنَ taktubna |
| هُم they (masc.) | | يَكْتُبُونَ yaktubuuna | يَكْتُبُوا* yaktubuu |
| هُنَّ they (fem.) | | يَكْتُبْنَ yaktubna | يَكْتُبْنَ yaktubna |

*Notice that the the masculine plurals have an extra *'alif* in the subjunctive. As with the past tense (see page 14), this *'alif* is silent.

# Irregular verbs in the subjunctive

Irregular verbs do not stray much from the rules for regular verbs in the subjunctive. There are some minor differences which you may meet occasionally:

- Weak verbs that end in a long *ii* ( ـِي ) or *uu* ( ـُو ) in the standard present tense, will end in *iya* ( ـِيَ ) or *uwa* ( ـُوَ ) in the subjunctive (if fully pronounced), but those that end in a long *aa* ( ـَى ) do not change:

  يَنْتَهِي *yantahii* – to finish – standard present tense →

  يَنْتَهِيَ *yantahiya* – *subjunctive*

  يَبْدُو *yabduu* – to seem/appear – standard present tense →

  يَبْدُوَ *yabduwa* – *subjunctive*

  يَنْسَى *yansaa* – to forget – standard present tense →

  يَنْسَى *yansaa* – *subjunctive* (no change)

# Uses of the subjunctive

The subjunctive is only used when verbs come after particular words (or "particles" as they are sometimes called). The most common of these is أَنْ (*'an* – to). Here is a fuller list, in rough order of frequency:

| | | |
|---|---|---|
| أَنْ | *'an* | to |
| (ألّا) | (*'allaa* | not to) |
| لِ | *li* | to/in order to |
| لَنْ | *lan* | shall/will not (used to make the future negative) |
| حَتّى | *Hatta\** | so that |
| لِكَيْ | *likayy* | in order to |

\* *Hatta* also means "until." The subjunctive is only used when it means "so that."

The structure أَنْ (*'an*) + *subjunctive* is used frequently in Arabic, often after verbs where in English we would use the infinitive (e.g., "can't run" or "want to vote").

لا أَسْتَطِيع أَنْ أَجْرِيَ مَعكُم اليَوْم لأَنِّي مَريض.

I can't run with you today because I'm sick.

هَلْ تُريدونَ أَنْ تُصَوِّتُوا في الإِنْتِخابات؟

Do you [*plural*] want to vote in the elections?

The other particles are used in roughly the same contexts as they would be in English:

عَلَيْكِ أن تُذاكِري لِتَنْجَحي في الامْتِحان.

You [*feminine*] should study [*lit:* "on you that you study"] in order to pass the exam.

هَيَا نَأْكُل الآن حَتَى نَنْتَهيَ قَبْلَ بداية البَرْنامِج.

Let's eat now so that we can finish before the start of the program.

لَنْ تَرَى القَمْر بالنَهار.

You won't see the moon in the daytime.

وَضَعْتُ الخِطابات في الأَظْرُف لِكَيْ أَرْسَلَها بالبَريد.

I put the letters in the envelopes in order to mail them.

# Summary of the *subjunctive*

- The *subjunctive* is a variation ("mood") of the present tense used after certain words.

- The most common of these words is أَنْ (*'an* – to).

- The *subjunctive* is very similar to the standard present tense for both regular and irregular verbs.

- The major difference affecting everyday usage and spelling is that the *nuun* (ن) is dropped from the end of the masculine plurals – تَكْتُبُوا/يَكْتُبُوا (*yaktubuu/taktubuu*) – and the feminine "you" – تَكْتُبي (*taktubii*).

# 1 3 Verbs in the jussive (incl. the imperative)

The *jussive* is the second variation of the present tense that you need to know. In many ways it is more important than the *subjunctive*, partly because it is more frequently used and partly because it displays more irregularities.

## Regular verbs in the jussive

In regular verbs, the *jussive*, like the *subjunctive*, is very similar to the standard present tense. Again like the *subjunctive*, the most significant change in regular verbs is that the *nuun* (ن) is dropped at the end of the masculine plurals — هُم (*hum*) and أَنْتُم ('*antum*) — and the feminine أَنْتِ ('*anti*) parts of the verb. (The dual is also affected — see Chapter 28).

The difference in regular verbs between the *subjunctive* and the *jussive* is that the *Damma* (ـُ) that ends many parts of the standard present tense (see page 15) changes to a *sukuun* (ـْ) in the *jussive*, rather than the *fatHa* (ـَ) of the *subjunctive*. In other words يَكْتُبُ (*yaktubu*) becomes يَكْتُبْ (*yaktub*) in the *jussive*. Since the standard present tense, the *subjunctive* and the *jussive* are all usually written without vowels and pronounced يَكْتُب (*yaktub*), you would not normally notice this change in regular verbs. (But it does become very significant in irregular verbs — see the section on page 70.)

The table on the next page shows the standard present tense and the *jussive* for the regular verb يَكْتُب *yaktub* (to write):

|  | **Standard present** | **Jussive** |
|---|---|---|
| *singular* | | |
| أَنَا I | أَكْتُبُ 'aktub(u) | أَكْتُبْ 'aktub |
| أَنْتَ you (masc.) | تَكْتُبُ taktub(u) | تَكْتُبْ taktub |
| أَنْتِ you (fem.) | تَكْتُبِينَ taktubiina | تَكْتُبِي taktubii |
| هُوَ he/it | يَكْتُبُ yaktub(u) | يَكْتُبْ yaktub |
| هِيَ she/it | تَكْتُبُ taktub(u) | تَكْتُبْ taktub |
| *plural* | | |
| نَحْنُ we | نَكْتُبُ naktub(u) | نَكْتُبْ naktub |
| أَنْتُمْ you (masc. pl) | تَكْتُبُونَ taktubuuna | تَكْتُبُوا* taktubuu |
| أَنْتُنَّ you (fem. pl) | تَكْتُبْنَ taktubna | تَكْتُبْنَ taktubna |
| هُم they (masc.) | يَكْتُبُونَ yaktubuuna | يَكْتُبُوا* yaktubuu |
| هُنَّ they (fem.) | يَكْتُبْنَ yaktubna | يَكْتُبْنَ yaktubna |

*Notice that the the masculine plurals have an extra *'alif* in the *jussive* as they do in the *subjunctive*. As with the past tense (see page 14), this *'alif* is silent.

# Irregular verbs in the *jussive*

The fact that the *jussive* ends in a *sukuun*, although largely insignificant in regular verbs, does have a big impact on many types of irregular verbs. Because the jussive replaces the *Damma* over the third root letter of many parts of the present tense with a *sukuun*, this can fundamentally affect the whole formation of many irregular verbs. The easiest way to approach this is to take each type of irregular verb in turn, as follows:

**Verbs with waaw or yaa' as a root letter**

• Verbs with waaw or yaa' as the first root letter (***assimilated verbs***) follow the same rules as regular verbs:

يَصِلُ *yaSil(u)* – he arrives (standard present tense)

يَصِلْ *yaSil* – he arrives (*jussive*)

• Verbs with *waaw* or *yaa'* as the second root letter (***hollow verbs***) change significantly in the *jussive*. These changes affect both the pronunciation and the spelling and so it is important to understand them. Firstly, remind yourself of the basic rules for hollow verbs (see pages 22–26 if you need more help):

> • **Sukuun** over third root letter of regular verb =
>   **short vowel** in the middle of irregular hollow verb
> • **Vowel** over third root letter of regular verb =
>   **long vowel** in the middle of irregular hollow verb

You know that a hollow verb in the standard present tense usually has a long vowel in the middle because the third root letter has a vowel over it — for example, يَزُورُ (*yazuur(u)* – he visits). In the *jussive*, however, the third root letter has a *sukuun* over it, and this means that a hollow verb will have a <u>short</u> vowel in the middle: يَزُرْ (*yazur*). Look at the table below showing how this rule applies to the other parts of the verb يَزُورُ . You could try covering the right-hand column and seeing if you can predict the jussive by looking at the rules above.

|  | | **Standard present** | **Jussive** |
|---|---|---|---|
| *singular* | | | |
| أنا | I | أَزُورُ 'azuur(u) | أَزُرْ 'azur |
| أَنْتَ | you (masc.) | تَزُورُ tazuur(u) | تَزُرْ tazur |
| أَنْتِ | you (fem.) | تَزُورِينَ tazuuriina | تَزُورِي tazurii |
| هُوَ | he/it | يَزُورُ yazuur(u) | يَزُرْ yazur |
| هِيَ | she/it | تَزُورُ tazuur(u) | تَزُرْ tazur |

|              | **Standard present** | **Jussive** |
|--------------|----------------------|-------------|
| *plural*     |                      |             |
| نَحْنُ we | نَزُورُ nazuur(u) | نَزُرْ nazur |
| أَنْتُمْ you (masc. pl) | تَزُورُونَ tazuuruuna | تَزُورُوا tazuuruu |
| أَنْتُنَّ you (fem. pl) | تَزُرْنَ tazurna | تَزُرْنَ tazurna |
| هُمْ they (masc.) | يَزُورُونَ yazuuruuna | يَزُورُوا yazuuruu |
| هُنَّ they (fem.) | يَزُرْنَ yazurna | يَزُرْنَ yazurna |

Notice that the feminine plurals are the only parts of the present tense that remain the same in the jussive. You can apply the pattern above to all hollow verbs, except that the short vowel will be *fatHa* (ـَ) if there is a long *aa* (ـا) in the standard present tense and *Kasra* (ـِ) if there is a long *ii* (ـِي):

يَبِيعُ *yabii*ε(*u*) – to sell – standard present tense →
يَبِعْ *yabi*ε – *jussive*

يَنَامُ *yanaam(u)* – to sleep – standard present tense →
يَنَمْ *yanam* – *jussive*

يُرِيدُ *yuriid(u)* – to want – standard present tense →
يُرِدْ *yurid* – *jussive*, etc.

• Verbs with *waaw* or *yaa'* as the third root letter (*defective verbs*) also change significantly in the *jussive*. These verbs often have a long vowel at the end of the standard present tense (see pages 28–29). This changes to a short vowel in the *jussive*. Defective verbs in the *jussive* can be awkward to spot since they often look like they only have two root letters, especially if you see them without vowels. Look at the standard present tense and the *jussive* for the verb يَمْشِي (*yamshii* – to walk):

|  | **Standard present** | **Jussive** |
|---|---|---|
| *singular* | | |
| أَنَا I | أَمْشِي 'amshii | أَمْشِ 'amshi |
| أَنْتَ you (masc.) | تَمْشِي tamshii | تَمْشِ tamshi |
| أَنْتِ you (fem.) | تَمْشِينَ tamshiina | تَمْشِي tamshii |
| هُوَ he/it | يَمْشِي yamshii | يَمْشِ yamshi |
| هِيَ she/it | تَمْشِي tamshii | تَمْشِ tamshi |
| *plural* | | |
| نَحْنُ we | نَمْشِي namshii | نَمْشِ namshi |
| أَنْتُمْ you (masc. pl) | تَمْشُونَ tamshuuna | تَمْشُوا tamshuu |
| أَنْتُنَّ you (fem. pl) | تَمْشِينَ tamshiina | تَمْشِينَ tamshiina |
| هُم they (masc.) | يَمْشُونَ yamshuuna | يَمْشُوا yamshuu |
| هُنَّ they (fem.) | يَمْشِينَ yamshiina | يَمْشِينَ yamshiina |

As with hollow verbs, this short vowel in the jussive of defective
verbs depends on the original long vowel:

يَنْتَهِي *yantahii* – to finish – standard present tense →
يَنْتَهِ *yantahi – jussive*

يَشْكُو *yashkuu* – to complain – standard present tense →
يَشْكُ *yashku – jussive*

يَنْسَى *yansaa* – to forget – standard present tense →
يَنْسَ *yansa – jussive*, etc.

## Doubled verbs

• The rule affecting whether the identical root letters are written
separately or together in a doubled verb is connected with the vowel

over the <u>third</u> root letter in a regular verb. Remind yourself of the
rule (see also Chapter 5):

---

- **Sukuun** over third root letter of regular verb =
  second and third root letters **written separately** in doubled verb
- **Vowel** over third root letter of regular verb =
  second and third root letters **written together** in doubled verb

---

The *sukuun* which characterizes much of the *jussive* means that the
second and third root letters are written separately more often than in
the standard present tense. Try covering the right-hand column of the
table below and predicting the *jussive* for the doubled verb يَرُدّ
(*yarudd* – to reply), applying the rules above.

|  |  | **Standard present** | **Jussive** |
|---|---|---|---|
| *singular* |  |  |  |
| أنا | I | أَرُدّ ʻarudd(u) | أَرْدُدْ ʻardud |
| أنْتَ | you (masc.) | تَرُدّ tarudd(u) | تَرْدُدْ tardud |
| أنْتِ | you (fem.) | تَرُدّينَ taruddiina | تَرُدّي taruddii |
| هُوَ | he/it | يَرُدّ yarudd(u) | يَرْدُدْ yardud |
| هِيَ | she/it | تَرُدّ tarudd(u) | تَرْدُدْ tardud |
| *plural* |  |  |  |
| نَحْنُ | we | نَرُدّ narudd(u) | نَرْدُدْ nardud |
| أنْتُمْ | you (masc. pl) | تَرُدّونَ tarudduuna | تَرُدّوا tarudduu |
| أنْتُنَّ | you (fem. pl) | تَرْدُدْنَ tardudna | تَرْدُدْنَ tardudna |
| هُم | they (masc.) | يَرُدّونَ yarudduuna | يَرُدّوا yarudduu |
| هُنَّ | they (fem.) | يَرْدُدْنَ yardudna | يَرْدُدْنَ yardudna |

**Verbs with *hamza* as a root letter**

• These verbs do not vary from regular verbs in the *jussive*. However, you should be aware of an alternative for the commonly used verb يَسْأَل (*yas'al* – to ask):

يَسْأَلُ *yas'al(u)* – to ask – standard present tense →

يَسْأَل *yas'al* OR يَسَلْ *yasal* – *jussive*

# Uses of the jussive

The *jussive* has three main uses in modern Arabic:

**Negative commands**

The *jussive* is used after لا (*laa*) to mean "don't" as an order or command:

لا تَزُرْ مَريضَك لأَكْثَر مِن نِصْف ساعة.

Don't visit your patient for more than half an hour.

لا تُحاوِلوا أَنْ تَتَسَلَّقوا هذِهِ الشَّجَرة العالية.

Don't [*plural*] try to climb this tall tree.

**fal (فَـ...) and li (لِـ...)**

The *jussive* is used after ...فَـ (*fal*), or less commonly ...لِ (*li*), with the meaning of "(so) let's:"

سَرَقَ اللُّصوص سَيّارَتنا! فَلْنَذهَبْ إلى الشُّرطة.

Thieves have stolen our car! So let's go to the police.

فَلْنَطْلُبْ مِن جيرانِنا أَنْ يَمْتَنِعوا عَنْ قَرْع الطُّبول.

Let's ask our neighbours to stop banging drums.

**Negative past**

The jussive is used after لَمْ (*lam*) to make the past tense negative ("didn't"):

لم أتزوّج بعد لأنني مفلس.

I haven't gotten married yet because I'm broke.

تأخّرت عمّتي لأنها لم تعثر على تاكسي.

My aunt was late because she didn't find a taxi.

لم يَنْتَهِ المُدير المالي مِنْ تَقْريره قَبْلَ الاجْتِماع.

The finance manager didn't finish his report before the meeting.

## The imperative

The *jussive* is also used as a base for forming the imperative, or commands. There are two basic categories and almost all Arabic verbs follow the rules for the appropriate category.

### Verbs with *sukuun* over the first root letter

If a verb has a *sukuun* over the first root letter in the jussive, the letters at the beginning (*prefix*) are taken off and replaced by an *'alif*:

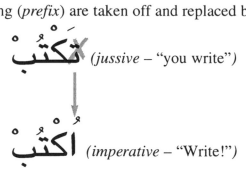

تَكْتُب (*jussive* – "you write")

اكْتُب (*imperative* – "Write!")

In a basic (form I) verb, the *'alif* on the front of the imperative will have a *Damma* if the middle vowel of the present is also a *Damma*, and a *kasra* if the middle vowel is either a *fatHa* or a *kasra*:

تَشْرَب *tashrab* – you drink (*jussive*) →
اشْرَب *ishrab* – Drink! (*imperative*)

تَطْلُبُوا *taTlubuu* – you [plural] request (*jussive*) →
أطْلُبُوا *uTlubuu* – Request! (*imperative*)

تَذْهَبِي *tadhhabii* – you [fem.] go (*jussive*) →
اذْهَبِي *idhhabii* – Go! (*imperative*)

Derived forms IV, VII, VII, and X also have a *sukuun* over the first root letter in the *jussive* and so have the added *'alif*. Form IV has a *fatHa* over the *'alif* and forms VII, VIII, and X all have a *kasra*:

تُرْسِل *tursil* – you send (*jussive, form IV*) →
أَرْسِل *arsil* – Send! (*imperative*)

تَسْتَعْلِمِي *tastaعlimii* – you [fem.] inquire (*jussive, form X*) →
اِسْتَعْلِمِي *istaعlimii* – Inquire! (*imperative*)

تَنْتَهِ *tantahi* – you finish (*jussive, form VIII*) →
اِنْتَهِ *intahi* – Finish! (*imperative*)

تَقْتَرِبوا *taqtaribuu* – you [pl.] approach (*jussive, form VIII*) →
اِقْتَرِبوا *iqtarib* – Approach! (*imperative*)

### Verbs with a vowel over the first root letter

Some verbs have a vowel over the first root letter of the *jussive*, rather than a sukuun. These type of verbs do not have the initial *'alif*:

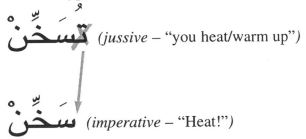

تُسْخِّنْ *(jussive – "you heat/warm up")*

سَخِّنْ *(imperative – "Heat!")*

Form II, III, V, and VI verbs are all like this, as are many irregular verbs, such as hollow verbs, doubled verbs, and verbs with *waaw* as the first root letter:

تَقُلْ *taqul* – you say (*jussive, hollow verb*) →
قُلْ *qul* – Say! (*imperative*)

تَتَذَكَّرْ *tatadhakkar* – you remember (*jussive, form V*) →
تَذَكَّرْ *tadhakkar* – Remember! (*imperative*)

تَرُدِّي *taruddii* – you [fem.] reply (*jussive, doubled verb*) →
رُدِّي *ruddii* – Reply! (*imperative*)

تَتَعَاوَنوا *tataعaawanuu* – you [pl.] cooperate (*jussive, form VI*) →
تَعَاوَنوا *taعaawanuu* – Cooperate! (*imperative*)

Here are some example sentences using the imperative:

تَعاوَنوا مَعاً في بِناء المَدْرَسة الجَديدة.

Cooperate in building the new school.

اِذْهَبي إلى الشاطِئ واسْبَحي مَعَ أصْدِقائِكِ.

Go [*fem.*] to the beach and swim with your friends.

اِشْرَب الشاي قَبْلَ أنْ يَبْرَد.

Drink the tea before it gets cold.

اُكْتُبْ اِسْمَك وعُنْوانك هُنا بِخَطّ واضِح.

Write your name and address here in clear handwriting.

ساعِدْني مِن فَضْلك لأنَّ هذا الصُّنْدوق ثَقيل.

Help me please because this box is heavy.

اِذْهَب إلى السوق واشْتَرِ لي بَعْضَ الفاكِهة.

Go to the market and buy me some fruit.

# Summary of the *jussive*

- The *jussive* is a variation ("mood") of the present tense used after certain words.

- The most common of these words are لا (*laa*) to mean "don't" as an order and لَمْ (*lam*) to make the past tense negative ("didn't").

- The *jussive* is very similar to the *subjunctive*. The difference is that there is a *sukuun* over the final root letter: يَكْتُبْ (*yaktub*), rather than a *fatHa* as in the *subjunctive*.

- The *sukuun* of the *jussive* changes the way many <u>irregular</u> verbs are written and pronounced. These need to be studied individually.

- The *jussive* is also used to form the imperative (orders), by removing the initial letters of the verb (up to the first root letter). If this leaves a *sukuun* over the first root letter, an *'alif* is added to the beginning.

# 14 Making verbs negative

This chapter contains a summary of how to make verbs negative. Some of these have been mentioned in previous chapters, but this summary will be a useful reference.

In English, we usually make verbs negative by adding the word "not," by itself or with another small helping word such as "do," "did," etc:

I walked → I did not walk.

I am going → I am not going.

I will find → I will not find.

I like → I do not like.

In Arabic, there are different ways of making a verb negative for different tenses. You need to remember each individually.

## Present tense

This is the simplest negative to form. You add the word لا (*laa*) in front of the standard present verb:

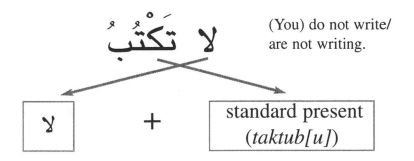

لا تَكْتُبُ    (You) do not write/ are not writing.

لا    +    standard present (*taktub[u]*)

## Past tense

The negative of the past tense is formed with لَمْ (*lam*) + *jussive*:

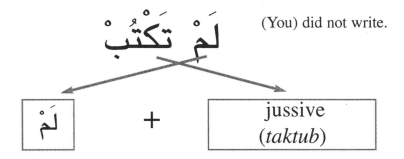

(You) did not write.

(See Chapter 13 for more details on the jussive.)

[It is possible you may see an alternative of the negative past tense formed by simply adding the word ما (*maa*) in front of the standard past: ما كَتَبْتَ (*maa katabta*). This is used less now in written Arabic but is still widespread in spoken dialects.]

## Future

The negative of the future is formed as follows:

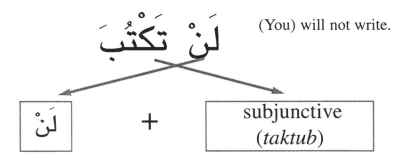

(You) will not write.

(See Chapter 12 for more details on the subjunctive.)

# Imperative (commands)

This is formed by using لا followed by the *jussive*:

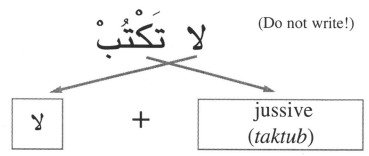

(Do not write!)

Be careful not to confuse this with the negative of the present tense.
Without the vowels, there may not always be a difference in the
spelling, but the context should tell you whether it is a command or not.

Here are some examples of the different negatives:

لا أُحِبُّ الاسْتِحْمام بالماء البارِد.

I don't like bathing with cold water.

لا تَلْعَبْ بالكَبْريت!

Don't play with matches!

كَلْبك لَنْ يَخونك أَبَداً.

Your dog will never betray you.

لَمْ نَتَّفِقْ لأَنَّهُ كان هُناك فَرْقٌ بَيْنَ رَأْينا ورأيكُم.

We didn't agree because there was a difference between
our viewpoint and yours.

لا تُغَنِّ يا أَخي لأَنَّ صَوتك مُزْعِج.

Don't sing ["O Brother"] because your voice is irritating.

النَّعامة طائِر لا يَطيرُ.

The ostrich is a bird [that] doesn't fly.

لَنْ تَنْتَهيَ فِترة الجَفاف إنْ لَمْ يَنْزِلْ* المَطَر.

The period of dry weather won't end if the rain doesn't* fall.

* After إنْ (if) Arabic uses the past tense.

# 15 Making verbs passive

Before we talk about the passive in Arabic, here is a quick reminder of what a passive sentence is. Look at these three sentences in English:

1  A spokesperson for the White House confirmed yesterday that the President was suffering from fatigue.

2  It was confirmed yesterday by a spokesperson for the White House that the President was suffering from fatigue.

3  It was confirmed yesterday that the President was suffering from fatigue.

All of these sentences mean the same. In the first two examples the subject of the verb ("A spokesperson for the White House") is present in the sentence. In sentence 1 the verb is active ("confirmed"); in sentence 2 the verb is passive ("It was confirmed"). The passive puts more emphasis on what is being confirmed rather than who is confirming — which is not so important in this case. In a passive sentence you can still include the subject after the word "by," but it is often omitted altogether, as in sentence 3.

Although you will see the passive from time to time in Arabic, it is not used as much as it is in English. This is partly because the English language is particularly fond of the passive and partly because Arabic has the derived form VII (يَنْفَعِل – *yanfaɛil*), which already has a passive meaning (see Chapter 10). You should be aware of the main features of the passive, but don't worry if you can't remember all the details.

## Passive of basic regular verbs

In English we use the verb "to be" + passive participle to form the passive (It was confirmed, They are sold, He has been caught, etc.). Arabic forms the passive by changing the vowels on the tenses. The past tense of a basic regular verb is vowelized in the passive with a *Damma* followed by a *kasra,* and the present tense with a *Damma* followed by a *fatHa.* This does not vary no matter what the vowels were originally on the active verb:

ذَكَرَ *Dhakara* – mentioned – active past tense →
ذُكِرَ *Dhukira* – was mentioned – passive past tense

شَرِبَ *shariba* – drank – active past tense →
شُرِبَ *shuriba* – was drunk – passive past tense

يَنْطِق *yanTuq[u]* – pronounces – active present tense →
يُنْطَق *yunTaq[u]* – is pronounced – passive present tense

يَضْرِب *yaDrib[u]* – hits – active present tense →
يُضْرَب *yuDrab[u]* – is hit – passive present tense

لا يُنْطَق حَرْف القاف في العَرَبِيَّة العامِيَّة المِصْرِيَّة.
The letter *qaaf* is not prounced in colloquial Egyptian Arabic.

سُرِقَتْ مِنِّي نُقودي!
My money has been stolen from me!

ذُكِرَ هذا الخَبَر في الرادْيو.
This news was mentioned on the radio.

يُشْرَب الشَّرْبات في الأفْراح.
Sherbet (cordial) is drunk at wedding celebrations.

طُلِبَ مِنِّي أَنْ أَكْتُب جُمَلاً لهذا الكِتاب.
I was asked to write sentences for this book.

# Irregular verbs in the passive

Irregular verbs follow the same basic vowelizing as for regular verbs in the passive, with some variations to fit in with the different patterns. Look at these table and examples:

|  | Active |  | Passive |  |
|---|---|---|---|---|

**Doubled verbs**

| past | عَدَّ | counted | عُدَّ | was counted |
|---|---|---|---|---|
| present | يَعُدّ | counts | يُعَدّ | is counted |

**Verbs with hamza**

*as 1st root letter:*

| past | أَمَرَ | commanded | أُمِرَ | was commanded |
|---|---|---|---|---|
| present | يَأْمُر | commands | يُؤْمَر | is commanded |

*as 2nd root letter:*

| past | سَأَلَ | asked | سُئِلَ | was asked |
|---|---|---|---|---|
| present | يَسْأَل | asks | يُسْأَل | is asked |

*as 3nd root letter:*

| past | قَرَأَ | read | قُرِئَ | was read |
|---|---|---|---|---|
| present | يَقْرَأ | read | يُقْرَأ | is read |

**Weak verbs**

*assimilated (1st root):*

| past | وَجَدَ | found | وُجِدَ | was found |
|---|---|---|---|---|
| present | يَجِد | finds | يُوجَد | is found |

*hollow (2nd root):*

| past | قال | said | قيل | was said |
|---|---|---|---|---|
| present | يَقول | says | يُقال | is said |

*defective (3rd root):*

| past | رَمَى | threw | رُمِيَ | was thrown |
|---|---|---|---|---|
| present | يَرْمي | throws | يُرْمَى | is thrown |

**Note:**

- The middle vowel of the passive reappears on a doubled verb if the second and third root letters are written separately, e.g. عُدِدْت (ع*udidtu*– I was counted/considered).
- When *hamza* is a root, the letter that carries the hamza can change in the passive as the vowels have changed (see page 34).
- Assimilated verbs have a long *uu* (و) sound at the beginning of the present passive.
- <u>All</u> hollow and weak verbs follow the same pattern in the passive, no matter what group they fall into.

راحة البال لا تقاس بالمال.

Peace of mind is not measured in money. (*Arabic proverb*)

أُعْلِمَ كُلّ مَن يُهِمُّهُ الأَمْر.

concerned [*lit:* whom the matter concerned] was informed. Everyone

قيلَ عَنْكَ كَلام كثير.

A lot [of talk] was said about you.

أَيْنَ توجَد المعابِد الأَثَرِيَّة؟

Where are the historic temples situated [*lit:* found]?

أُمِرَ الجَيش بالهُجوم.

# Derived forms in the passive

The derived forms are very similar to the basic verb in the passive, with all tenses starting vowelized initially with a *Damma*. Like the basic verb, the second root letter carries a *kasra* in the past passive and a *fatHa* in the present passive in all the derived forms. Around these vowels, there are some minor variations as shown below:

| Derived Form | Past passive | | Present passive | |
|---|---|---|---|---|
| II | كُسِّرَ | was smashed | يُكَسَّر | is smashed |
| III | عُومِلَ | was treated | يُعامَل | is treated |
| IV | أُعْلِمَ | was informed | يُعْلَم | is informed |
| V | تُوُقِّعَ | was expected | يُتَوَقَّع | is expected |
| VI | تُحُودِثَ | was discussed | يُتَحادَث | is discussed |
| VII* | — | — | — | — |
| VIII | أُحْتُرِمَ | was respected | يُحْتَرَم | is respected |
| X | أُسْتُخْرِجَ | was extracted | يُسْتَخْرَج | is extracted |

*Form VII has a passive meaning anyway and is virtually never seen in the passive form.

عُومِلَ المَريض بِعِناية بَعْدَ الجِراحة.

The patient was treated with care after the surgery.

أُعْلِمَ كُلّ مَن يُهِمُّهُ الأَمْر.

Everyone concerned [*lit:* whom the matter concerned] was informed.

يُتَوَقَّع أَنْ يَسْقُط المَطَر بَعْد يَوْمَيْن.

Rain is expected to fall in two days.

يُسْتَخْرَج الذَّهَب مِن المَناجِم.

[The] gold is extracted from [the] mines.

# Summary of the passive

- The passive is not as common in Arabic as in English, but you will meet it from time to time.

- The most significant indicator of the passive is the *Damma* (ُ) at the beginning of both the past and present verbs.

- In the past passive, there is also a *kasra* under the second root letter: فُعِلَ (*fuɛila*).

- In the present passive, there is also a *fatHa* over the second root letter: يُفْعَل (*yufɛal*).

- Irregular verbs and derived forms are variations on the patterns above but need to be referenced individually.

# 16 Verbal nouns & other verbal constructions

The first fifteen chapters of this book cover the main tenses, variations and derivations of Arabic verbs. This chapter covers verbal nouns and other constructions that are derived from verbs. These follow more or less predictable patterns. Connecting these patterns with a particular type of construction and meaning will help you to further expand your vocabulary and understand the structure of Arabic.

## Verbal nouns

In English we make nouns from verbs by adding endings such as "-tion," "-ment," or "-ing" (e.g., "information," "treatment, " "swimming," etc.). Arabic puts the root letters into different patterns to make verbal nouns. These are widely used and you should try to remember the main patterns and uses.

### Nouns from basic verbs

Unfortunately as far as the learner is concerned, basic verbs have many different patterns for forming verbal nouns. Here are some of the more common patterns with examples:

| Pattern | Example |
|---|---|
| فَعْل (faعl) | ضَرْب (Darb – hitting) from يَضْرِب (yaDrib) |
| فُعول (fuعuul) | دُخُول (dukhuul – entering) from يَدْخُل (yadkhul) |
| فَعال (faعaal) | ذَهاب (dhahaab – going) from يَذْهَب (yadhhab) |
| فِعالة (fiعaala) | سِباحة (sibaaHa – swimming) from يَسْبَح (yasbaH) |
| فَعَل (faعal) | عَمَل (عamal – working) from يَعْمَل (yaعmal) |

However, there are many more patterns for basic verbs, and you will need to look each one up individually in a dictionary. The verbal noun is usually listed together with the verb.

Because of the numerous variations in the way verbal nouns are formed, it is also difficult to generalize about irregular verbs. Some types of irregular verb will behave regularly in some patterns and irregularly in others. Only by looking up and remembering each verbal noun individually will you start to get a feel for how irregular verbs behave and start to take guesses at the likely patterns.

### Verbal nouns from derived forms

Verbal nouns from derived forms are much more predictable. Only form III has a widely used alternative. Generally, if you know which derived form a verb is, you will be able to create the verbal noun without reference to a dictionary. The table below shows the verbal noun for the derived forms:

| Derived Form | Present verb | | Verbal noun | |
|---|---|---|---|---|
| II | يُكَسِّر | smashes up | تَكْسِير | smashing up |
| III* | يُعامِل | treats | مُعامَلة | treatment |
| IV | يُعْلِم | informs | إعْلام | information |
| V | يَتَوَقَّع | expects | تَوَقُّع | expectation |
| VI | يَتَعاوَن | cooperating | تَعاوُن | cooperation |
| VII | يَنْقَلِب | overturns | اِنْقِلاب | overturning |
| VIII | يَحْتَرِم | respects | اِحْتِرام | respect |
| X | يَسْتَحْسِن | admires | اِسْتِحْسان | admiration |

The alternative verbal noun for form III is فِعال as in بِدال (*bidaal* – exchanging).

**Uses of verbal nouns**

• Generalizations

Verbal nouns are used for generalizing, much as they are in English. Note that you need to include ...الـَ (*al* – the) in Arabic.

السِّبـاحة مُفيدة لصِّحّتك.

Swimming is beneficial to your health.

الانقِلابـات تَسْعَى لِتَغْيير الحُكومات.

Coups attempt to change governments.

الفَنّانونَ يُحاولونَ أَنْ يُنالوا اِسْتِحْسان الجُمْهور.

Artists try to gain the admiration of the public.


• In place of أَنْ ( *'an*) + *subjunctive*

Arabic does not have an infinitive like the English "to walk," "to see," etc. Chapter 12 shows how أَنْ ( *'an*) + *subjunctive* can be used in Arabic where English would use an infinitive. Another common alternative is to use the verbal noun. Look at these two sentences, which have the same meaning. The first uses أَنْ ( *'an*) + *subjunctive* (أَذهَبَ) and the second a verbal noun with *al* (الذَهاب):

أَوَدّ أَنْ أَذهَبَ إلَى السُّوق.

أَوَدّ الذَهـاب إلَى السُّوق.

I'd like to go to the market.


It is considered good style to use verbal nouns in this way and is often less clumsy than using a repeating أَنْ. Look at the sentences below and also watch for this usage in authentic Arabic.

زَوجي يُريد المُقامرة بمـالي أنا!

My husband wants to gamble with <u>my</u> money!

أَرْفَض الدُخول في مُناقشات عَميقة.

I refuse to enter into deep discussions.

• Together with a verb

A verbal noun can be used together with the equivalent verb to add information about the action:

زرْتُ أُمِّي زِيارة قَصيرة

I visited my mother for a short time [*lit:* a short visit]

طُلِبَتْ مِنِّي طَلَبات كَثيرة كلّها صَعْبة.

Many requests have been asked of me, all of them difficult.

تَعاوَنوا مَعَنا تَعاوُناً مُثْمِراً.

They cooperated with us successfully.

In addition, many verbal nouns have also acquired a specific meaning in general circulation. For example, the word خِطاب (*khitaab*) now means "a letter" but is originally the verbal noun from ("to address publicly").

# Active and passive participles

An active participle is the equivalent of the English "-ing," as in "I went along the road, <u>whistling</u> a tune."(i.e., <u>I</u> was whistling.) A passive participle is the equivalent of the English "burned" as in "I found the cakes in the oven, <u>burned</u> to a cinder." (i.e., The cakes <u>had been</u> burned.) These can also be used as adjectives to describe something: "a whistling machine," "burnt toast," etc. In Arabic, the active and passive participles are also used to mean "the person/thing that [whistles]" and "the person/thing that is [burned]."

### Basic verbs

The active participle is formed by taking the root letters and putting them into the pattern فاعِل (*faaɛil*):

كاتِب (*kaatib*) writing/writer

لاعِب (*laaɛib*) playing/player

راكِب (*raakib*) riding/rider

The passive participle is formed by putting the root letters into the pattern مَفْعول (*mafɛuul*):

مَسْجُون (*masjuun*) imprisoned/prisoner

مَنْدُوب (*manduub*) delegated/delegate

مكْسُور (*maksuur*) [thing] broken

Don't forget that the examples above only refer to one masculine
person or object. If you want to refer to a female or a group, you will
need to add the appropriate ending; for example, كاتِبة (*kaatiba*) would
be a female writer and لاعِبون (*laaɛibuun*) would be a group of players.
See Chapters 21 and 22 for more detail on these endings.

Irregular verbs show some variations when put into the patterns for the
active and passive participles:

### Doubled verbs

| | | |
|---|---|---|
| active participle | سادّ | blocking |
| passive participle | مَسْدود | [thing] blocked |

### Verbs with hamza

*as 1st root letter:*

| | | |
|---|---|---|
| active participle | آمِر | commanding/commander |
| passive participle | مَأْمور | [person] commanded |

*as 2nd root letter:*

| | | |
|---|---|---|
| active participle | سائِل | asking/asker |
| passive participle | مَسْؤُول | [person] asked |

*as 3nd root letter:*

| | | |
|---|---|---|
| active participle | قارِئ | reading/reader |
| passive participle | مَقْروء | [thing] read |

### Weak verbs

*assimilated (1st root):*

| | | |
|---|---|---|
| active participle | واجد | finding/finder |
| passive participle | مَوْجود | [thing] found |

*hollow (2nd root):*

| | | |
|---|---|---|
| active participle | بائِع | buying/buyer |
| passive participle | مَبيع/مَقول* | [thing] sold/[thing] said |

*defective (3rd root):*

| | | |
|---|---|---|
| active participle | قاض** | judging/judge |
| passive participle | مَقْضِيّ/مَدْعُوّ* | [person] judged/invited |

* Alternatives are given for verbs with *waaw* as the root letter.
** Pronounced *qaaDin*. A *yaa'* reappears in the definite: القاضي (*al-qaaDii*)

**Active and passive participles in the derived forms**

Active and passive participles in the derived forms are similar across
all the forms and also very similar to each other. All the active and
passive participles for derived forms begin with the prefix ـُﻣ (*mu*).
After that, the vowelizing is the same as the present tense for the active
participle, with the *kasra* under the second root letter changing to a
*fatHa* for the passive participle. This means that the only thing that
separates the active participle مُفَتِّش (*mufattish* – inspector) from the
passive particle مُفَتَّش (*mufattash* – inspected) is a single vowel.
Because of this, you will often find that this vowel will be included for
clarity, even on texts that are otherwise not vowelized.

| Derived Form | Active participle | | Passive participle | |
|---|---|---|---|---|
| II | مُفَتِّش | inspecting/inspector | مُفَتَّش | inspected |
| III | مُعاوِن | helping/helper | مُعاوَن | helped |
| IV | مُرْسِل | sending/sender | مُرْسَل | sent |
| V | مُتَوَقِّع | expecting | مُتَوَقَّع | expected |
| VI | مُتَفارِق | dispersing | مُتَفارَق | dispersed |
| VII | مُنْصَرِف | departing | مُنْصَرَف | departed |
| VIII | مُحْتَرِم | respecting | مُحْتَرَم | respected |
| X | مُسْتَعْمِل | utilizing | مُسْتَعْمَل | utilized |

Here are some example sentences showing active and passive
participles in context:

الشيكات المُرْسلة بالبَريد تَأَخَّرَتْ في الوُصول.

The checks that were mailed were late in arriving.

كُلّ مُسْتَعْمِل لِهذا النَفَق يُخْتَصِر مِن رِحْلتِهِ ساعتَين.

Every user of this tunnel cuts two hours from his journey.

تَجَوَّلَت المُفَتِّشات بَيْنَ الفُصول في المَدْرَسة.

The [female] inspectors alternated between classrooms in the school.

إِشْتَرَيْنا كُلّ الخُبْز المَوْجود في المَخْبَز.

We bought all the bread found in the bakery.

سارِقو البَنْك كانوا مِن المُحْتَرِفين.

Those who robbed the bank were professionals.

# Nouns of place and instrument

Another nouns that are derived from verbs are *nouns of place* and *nouns of instrument*.

Nouns of place describe the place where an action happens. They are formed by putting root letters of a verb into the pattern مَفْعَل (*mafεal*), مَفْعِل (*mafεil*), or مَفْعَلة (*mafεala*):

مَدْرَسة (*madrasa* – school ["place of study"])  from يدرس (to study)

مكْتَب (*maktab* – desk/office ["place of writing"]) from يكتب (to write)

مَصْنَع (*maSnaε* – factory ["place of manufacture"]) from يصنع (to manufacture)

مَجْلِس (*majlis* – council ["place of sitting"]) from يجلس (to sit)

Nouns of instrument describe the implement used to perform an action. They are formed by putting the root letter of a verb into the pattern مِفْعَل (*mifεal*), مِفْعال (*mifεaal*), or مِفْعَلة (*mifεala*):

مِفْتاح (*miftaH* – key ["instrument of opening"]) from يفتح (to open)

مِكْنَسة (*miknasa* – broom ["instrument of sweeping"]) from يكنس (to sweep)

مِقَصّ (*miqaSS* – scissors ["instrument of cutting"]) from يقصّ (to cut)

مِنْشار (*minshaar* – saw ["instrument of sawing"])  from ينشر (to saw)

# Summary of verbal nouns and other verbal constructions

- There are a number of nouns and participles that can be formed from verbs. The most important of these are verbal nouns, active and passive participles, nouns of place, and nouns of instrument. Familiarizing yourself with the patterns connected to each of these will help you expand your vocabulary.

- Verbal nouns are formed from the root letters of a verb using a variety of patterns. These patterns are more predictable in the derived forms than the basic form. Verbal nouns are mainly used for generalizations and in sentences where English would use the infinitive (to walk/see, etc.)

- Active participles follow the pattern فاعِل (*faaɛil*) in the basic verb. In the derived forms they all start with the sound مُـ (*mu*) and have a *kasra* as the final vowel. They are the rough equivalent of the English "-ing," but can also be used to describe the person/thing carrying out an action.

- Passive participles follow the pattern مَفْعُول (*mafɛuul*) in the basic verb. In the derived forms they are the same as the active participle, except that they have *fatHa* as the final vowel. They are the equivalent of the English past participle (burned/drunk, etc.), but can also be used to describe the person/thing which is the object of an action.

- There are also patterns which are used to describe the place or instrument of an action. Nouns of place start with مـ (*ma*) and nouns of instrument with مـ (*mi*). The vowels after this vary and each word should be learned individually.

# 17 Verbs in the dual

Arabic distinguishes between two things or people (the *dual*) and more than two (the *plural*). Chapter 28 gives a more detailed overview of the dual, but this chapter specifically looks at the dual verb endings.

The dual verb endings have been deliberately separated so that you can tackle them only when you are confident with other aspects and types of the verb.

There are three different dual endings for the following:

أنتُما (*'antumaa*: you two – both masculine and feminine)

هُما (*humaa*: they two – masculine*)

هُما (*humaa*: they two – feminine*)

*Note that although the word for the dual "they" is هُما (*humaa*) for both masculine and feminine, the verb endings are different.

Here are the dual endings for the verb كَتَب/يَكْتُب (to write):

|  | **Past** | **Present** | **Subjunctive*** | **Jussive*** |
|---|---|---|---|---|
| أنْتُما | كَتَبْتُما<br>(*katabtumaa*) | تَكْتُبان<br>(*taktubaani*) | تَكْتُبا<br>(*taktubaa*) | تَكْتُبا<br>(*taktubaa*) |
| هُما (*masc.*) | كَتَبا<br>(*katabaa*) | يَكْتُبان<br>(*yaktubaani*) | يَكْتُبا<br>(*yaktubaa*) | يَكْتُبا<br>(*yaktubaa*) |
| هُما (*fem.*) | كَتَبَتا<br>(*katabataa*) | تَكْتُبان<br>(*taktubaani*) | تَكْتُبا<br>(*taktubaa*) | تَكْتُبا<br>(*taktubaa*) |

* Note that the dual loses the final *nuun* in the subjunctive and jussive as the masculine plurals do.

\_gular verbs will follow the same rules in the dual as those for other parts of the verb. Also note that, like the plural, a verb will only be dual if it comes <u>after</u> the subject; otherwise it will be singular (see page 63 for more details.)

العائِلتان هـاجَرَتا إلى كَنَدا بَعْدَ الحَرْب.

The two families emigrated to Canada after the war.

هذان الفيلان يَشْتركان في عُروض السيرْك.

These two elephants take part in the circus parades.

تُريد اِبْنَتايَ أَنْ تَتَفَوَّقا في اِمْتِحان اللُّغة الفَرَنْسِيَّة.

My two daughters want to succeed in the French language examination.

# 18 Verbs with four root letters (quadriliterals)

Most Arabic verbs have three root letters, but there are a few that have four. These verbs are called *quadriliteral* ( رُباعي ). A few of these verbs are reasonably common and you will need to recognize them.

## Basic quadrititeral verb

A basic quadriliteral verb is vowelized very similarly to form II of a *triliteral* verb (verb with three root letters.) The past tense is vowelized with all *fatHas* and the present with *Damma/fatHa/kasra*:

**Past tense:** دَحْرَجَ *(daHraja)* – rolled
**Present tense:** يُدَحْرِج *(yudaHrij)* – rolls

The active and passive participles are also very similar to form II:

**Active participle:** مُدَحْرِج *(mudaHrij)* – rolling
**Passive participle:** مُدَحْرَج *(mudaHraj)* – (been) rolled

The most common verbal noun from a basic quadriliteral verb is دَحْرَجة *(daHraja)*, although some minor variations exist.

Many verbs with four root letters are in fact created by repeating the same sequence of two letters. This is often used for *onomatopoeic* verbs (verbs that sound similar to their meaning:)

يُثَرْثِر *(yutharthir)* – to chatter
يُغَرْغِر *(yugharghir)* – to gargle
يُتَمْتِم *(yutamtim)* – to stammer
يُدَنْدِن *(yudandin)* – to hum

# Derived forms of quadriliteral verbs

In theory, there are three derived forms for quadriliteral verbs. In practice, form III is virtually extinct and there are no more than a handful of verbs in the other two forms in common circulation. However, for the sake of these verbs, here are the past and present tenses for forms II and IV of quadriliteral verbs:

## Form II

**Past tense:** تَفَلْسَفَ (*tafalsafa*) – philosophized
**Present tense:** يَتَفَلْسَف (*yatafalsaf*) – philosophizes

## Form IV

**Past tense:** اِقْشَعَرَّ (*iqshaعarra*) – shuddered/quaked
**Present tense:** يَقْشَعِرّ (*yaqshaعirr*) – shudders/quakes

Here are some examples of quadriliteral verbs in context:

أُدَنْدِن تَحْتَ الدُش.
I hum in [*lit:* under] the shower.

أَنْتِ تُثَرْثِرينَ عَلَى التَليفون مُنْذُ الصَباح.
You [*fem.*] have been chattering on the telephone since the morning.

تَسَلْسَلَتْ أَحْداث الفيلْم بِإيقاع سَريع.
The events of the film followed one another at a fast pace.

الخَشَب الرَطِب يُطَقْطِق في المَدْفَأة.
Damp wood crackles in the fireplace.

# 19 Some very unusual common verbs

A few verbs have particular oddities, usually because of multiple combinations of irregular features. The most important of these are listed below. Since they are some of the most common verbs in the Arabic language, you will need to try and memorize them individually.

## جاء/يجيء (to come)

This verb represents the most common group of very irregular verbs: hollow verbs that also have *hamza* as the last root letter. Both the rules applying to hollow verbs and the rules for the spelling of *hamza* apply to these verbs, causing multiple changes.

| singular | Past | | Present | | Subjunctive | | Jussive | |
|---|---|---|---|---|---|---|---|---|
| أنا | جِئْتُ | (ji'tu) | أَجِيءُ | ('ajii'[u]) | أَجِيءَ | ('ajii'[a]) | أَجِئْ | (aji') |
| أنْتَ | جِئْتَ | (ji'ta) | تَجِيءُ | (tajii'[u]) | تَجِيءَ | (tajii'[a]) | تَجِئْ | (taji') |
| أنْتِ | جِئْتِ | (ji'ti) | تَجِيئِينَ | (tajii'iina) | تَجِيئِي | (tajii'ii) | تَجِيئِي | (tajii'ii) |
| هُوَ | جاءَ | (jaa'a) | يَجِيءُ | (yajii'[u]) | يَجِيءَ | (yajii'[a]) | يَجِئْ | (yaji') |
| هِيَ | جاءَتْ | (jaa'at) | تَجِيءُ | (tajii'[u]) | تَجِيءَ | (tajii'[a]) | تَجِئْ | (taji') |
| **plural** | | | | | | | | |
| نَحْنُ | جِئْنا | (ji'naa) | نَجِيءُ | (najii'[u]) | نَجِيءَ | (najii'[a]) | نَجِئْ | (naji') |
| أنْتُمْ | جِئْتُمْ | (ji'tum) | تَجِيئُونَ | (tajii'uuna) | تَجِيئُوا | (tajii'uu) | تَجِيئُوا | (tajii'uu) |
| أنْتُنَّ | جِئْتُنَّ | (ji'tunna) | تَجِئْنَ | (taji'na) | تَجِئْنَ | (taji'na) | تَجِئْنَ | (taji'na) |
| هُمْ | جاءوا | (jaa'uu) | يَجِيئُونَ | (yajii'uuna) | يَجِيئُوا | (yajii'uu) | يَجِيئُوا | (yajii'uu) |
| هُنَّ | جِئْنَ | (ji'na) | يَجِئْنَ | (yaji'na) | يَجِئْنَ | (yaji'na) | يَجِئْنَ | (yaji'na) |

جاءوا إلى بَيتي بَعْدَ خُروجي.

They came to my house after I had left [*lit*: after my leaving].

لَمْ أَجِئْ لأَنِّي مَريض.

I didn't come because I'm sick.

## رأى/يرى (to see)

This verb has the root letters ر (*raa'*) + ء (*hamza*) + ي (*yaa'*). It acts relatively normally in the past, but drops the *hamza* altogether in the present. Pay particular attention to the *jussive*. The *yaa'* also gets dropped, which makes for a very short verb!

| singular | **Past** | | **Present** | | **Subjunctive** | | **Jussive** | |
|---|---|---|---|---|---|---|---|---|
| أنا | رَأَيْتُ | (ra'aytu) | أَرَى | ('araa) | أَرَى | ('araa) | أَرَ | ('ara) |
| أنْتَ | رَأَيْتَ | (ra'ayta) | تَرَى | (taraa) | تَرَى | (taraa) | تَرَ | (tara) |
| أنْتِ | رَأَيْتِ | (ra'ay'ti) | تَرَيْنَ | (tarayna) | تَرَيْ | (taray) | تَرَيْ | (taray) |
| هُوَ | رَأَى | (ra'aa) | يَرَى | (yaraa) | يَرَى | (yaraa) | يَرَ | (yara) |
| هِيَ | رَأَتْ | (ra'at) | تَرَى | (taraa) | تَرَى | (taraa) | تَرَ | (tara) |
| *plural* | | | | | | | | |
| نَحْنُ | رَأَيْنا | (ra'aynaa) | نَرَى | (naraa) | نَرَى | (naraa) | نَرَ | (nara) |
| أنْتُمْ | رَأَيْتُمْ | (ra'aytum) | تَرَوْنَ | (tarauna) | تَرَوْا | (tarau) | تَرَوْا | (tarau) |
| أنْتُنَّ | رَأَيْتُنَّ | (ra'aytunna) | تَرَيْنَ | (tarayna) | تَرَيْنَ | (tarayna) | تَرَيْنَ | (tarayna) |
| هُم | رَأَوْا | (ra'au) | يَرَوْنَ | (yarauna) | يَرَوْا | (yarau) | يَرَوْا | (yarau) |
| هُنَّ | رَأَيْنَ | (ra'ayna) | يَرَيْنَ | (yarayna) | يَرَيْنَ | (yarayna) | يَرَيْنَ | (yarayna) |

هَلْ رَأَيْتَ آلة الطّباعة الجَديدة في المَعْرَض؟

Did you see the new printing machine at the exhibition?

أُريد أَنْ أَرى أُمّي.

I want to see my mother.

لَمْ يَرَ الزبون المَصْنَع الجَديد أَمْس.

The client didn't see the new factory yesterday.

## لَيْسَ (not to be)

Arabic does not have a verb "to be" (is/are/am, etc.) in simple positive sentences (see Chapter 23 for more details.) However, it does have a verb "not to be." The sentence:

هـاني طَبيب. Haanii (is) a doctor.

can be made negative by adding لَيْسَ or لَيْسَ...بِـ:

لَيْسَ هـاني طَبيباً*. Haanii isn't a doctor.

لَيْسَ هـاني بطَبيب. Haanii isn't a doctor.

* طبيب now has the accusative ending طَبيباً (*Tabiiban*) – see Appendix (ii).

لَيْسَ is unusual because it looks like a past verb, but always has a present meaning ("Haani wasn't a doctor" would be لَمْ يَكُنْ هـاني طبيباً). However, it does change according to the subject:

لَسْتُ I'm not

لَسْتَ/لَسْتِ/لَسْتُمْ you're not

لَيْسَ he's not

لَيْسَتْ she's not

لَسْنَ we're not

لَيْسوا/لَسْنَ they're not

المُوَظَّفون لَيْسوا في المَكْتَب قَبْلَ الساعة التاسِعة.

The employees are not in the office before nine o'clock.

لَسْتُ بمُدَرِّس.

I'm not a teacher.

# Part Two:
## *Essentials of Grammar*

# 20 The article and personal pronouns

## اَلـ al (*definite article*)

Arabic does not have an equivalent of the English "a/an" (indefinite article) as in "a book/an apple," The word is simply written by itself:

كِتاب (*kitaab*) a book

بِنْت (*bint*) a girl

مُدَرِّس (*mudarris*) a teacher

However, there is an equivalent of "the" (*definite article*): اَلـ (*al*). This is joined to the beginning of the word, rather than written separately.

اَلْكِتاب (*al-kitaab*) the book

اَلْبِنْت (*al-bint*) the girl

اَلْمُدَرِّس (*al-mudarris*) the teacher

The *fatHa* (*a*) is dropped from *al* when the previous word ends in a vowel:

وَجَدَ الْكِتاب. (*wajada l-kitaab*) He found the book.

هذِهِ الْبِنْت (*haadhihi l-bint*) this girl

Sometimes, the *lam* (ل) of the word اَلـ is pronounced the same as the first letter of the word that follows:

اَلسَّيّارة (*as-sayyara*) the car

اَلرَّجُل (*ar-rajul*) the man

اَلتُّفّاحة (*at-tuffaHa*) the apple

Notice how the first letter of the word now has a *shadda* (ـّ) over it to show that it is doubled. There are fourteen letters in Arabic that cause *al* to change. These letters are called "sun letters" ( الحُروف الشَّمْسيّة), and you can find a full list of them in Appendix (i). Pronouncing these correctly is something that will take experience and time but will eventually become automatic.

# Personal pronouns

Personal pronouns are the equivalent of the English "I/we/you/she/he," etc. These are:

> *singular*
>
> أنا (*'ana*) I
>
> أنْتَ (*'anta*) you [*masculine*]
>
> أنْتِ (*'anti*) you [*feminine*]
>
> هُوَ (*huwa*) he/it
>
> هِيَ (*hiya*) she/it
>
> *plural*
>
> نَحْنُ (*naHnu*) we
>
> أنْتُمْ (*'antum*) you [*pl. masculine*]
>
> أنْتُنَّ (*'antunna*) you [*pl. feminine*]
>
> هُمْ (*hum*) they [*masculine*]
>
> هُنَّ (*hunna*) they [*feminine*]

(The next chapter explains more about feminine and masculine.)


Note that Arabic also has different pronouns for "you" and "they" when talking about two people (*the dual*). See Chapter 28 for details on these.

# 21 Genders

Arabic, like many other languages, makes a difference between male and female nouns (people, objects, ideas, etc.) It has two *genders*: *masculine* (male) and *feminine* (female). The gender of a noun will affect other words in a sentence, such as verbs, adjectives, etc., so you need to be confident in this aspect of the grammar.

Luckily, <u>unlike</u> many other languages, it is usually easy to tell the difference between masculine and feminine nouns in Arabic. There are only a few exceptions to the general rules.

There are two main categories of feminine words:

**Words that refer to females — e.g.,:**

بِنْت (*bint*) girl

أُمّ (*'umm*) mother

لَيْلَى (*layla*) Layla (or any other girl's name)

Note that most countries are also feminine nouns.

**Words that end in ة (*ta' marbuuTa*):**

There is a special feminine ending that is a cross between ت (*taa'*) and ه (*ha'*): ة. This is called *ta' marbuuTa*. The vowel before a *ta' marbuuTa* is always a *FatHa*. Words that end with *ta' marbuuTa* are almost always feminine.

مَدينَة (*madiina*) city

مَكْتَبَة (*maktaba*) bookstore

فِكْرة (*fikra*) idea

Usually, the *ta' marbuuTa* is not pronounced — only the *fatHa* that comes before it.

There are many feminine words that fit into both of the categories above, ending in *ta' marbuuTa* <u>and</u> referring to female people:

زَوْجة (*zawja*) wife

مُمَرِضَّة (*mumariDDa*) [female] nurse

خالة (*khaala*) [maternal] aunt

There are also a few feminine words that do not fit into either category. Most of these are parts of the body or are connected with the natural world. Here are some examples of these.

شَمْس (*shams*) sun

يَد (*yad*) hand

أَرْض (*'arD*) earth

رِجْل (*rijl*) foot

In general, however, you can assume a word is masculine unless it refers to a female or ends in *ta' marbuuTa*.

# 22 Sentences without verbs

In Arabic, the verb "to be" (e.g., I <u>am</u>, you <u>are</u>, he <u>is</u>, etc.) is omitted in simple present sentences. This means that in Arabic, unlike in English, you can have a sentence with no verb at all:

أَحْمَد مُدَرِّس. Ahmed (is a) teacher.

أَنا مَشْغول اليَوم. I (am) busy today.

أُمّي في الحَمـام. My mother (is) in the bathroom.

الشُّبـاك مَكْسور. The window (is) broken.

These types of sentences are called "nominal sentences."

## Demonstrative pronouns

You will often find nominal sentences using the Arabic equivalents of "this" and "that" (*demonstrative pronouns*):

هـٰذا (*haadhaa*)  this (masculine singular)
هـٰذِهِ (*haadhihi*)  this (feminine singular)
هـٰؤُلاءِ (*haa'ulaa'i*)  these (plural*)

ذٰلِكَ (*dhaalika*)  that (masculine singular)
تِلْكَ (*tilka*)  that (feminine singular)
أُولـٰئِكَ (*'ulaa'ika*)  those (plural*)

*The plurals are only used for people. For nonhuman plurals, use the feminine singular — see Chapter 23.

هذا كِتاب.   This (is a) book.

هذِهِ أُخْتي.   This (is) my sister.

تِلكَ أُمّي.   That (is) my mother.

هَؤُلاءِ مُوَظَّفون في شَرِكتي.   These (are) employees in my company.

Be careful to distinguish between the following:

هذا كِتاب.   (*haadhaa kitaab*) This (is) a book.

هذا الكِتاب...   (*haadhaa l-kitaab*) This book...

The first is a sentence, the second is not. You need to add the appropriate pronoun, in this case هو (*huwa*), if you want to say the sentence "This is the book.", :

هذا هُوَ الكِتاب.   (*haadhaa huwa l-kitaab*) This (is) the book.

هذِهِ هيَ المُشْكِلة.   (*haadhihi hiya l-mushkila*) This (is) the problem.

You should include the appropriate form of the verb يكون (*yakuun*) if a sentence requires you to use the *subjunctive, jussive,* or *imperative* (see Chapters 12 and 13 for when these are used):

أَحْمَد يُريد أَنْ يكون مُدَرِّساً.   Ahmed wants to be a teacher.

كُنْ لَطيفاً مَعَ أُخْتِكَ.   Be gentle with your sister.

لا تكونوا كَسالَى.   Don't be [*plural*] lazy.

If you want to make a nominal sentence negative, you need to use the special verb لَيْسَ (see page 101).

# 23 Describing things (adjectives)

Adjectives are the words you use to describe something, such as the English "happy," "heavy," "red," "busy," etc. In English, adjectives come <u>before</u> the person or thing described (the *noun*) and do not change depending on whether the noun is singular or plural, etc.:

a happy baby
happy babies
a red light
red lights

In Arabic, adjectives come <u>after</u> the noun and change depending on whether the noun is singular or plural, masculine or feminine.

## Masculine and feminine adjectives

If the noun described is feminine, then the adjective is also feminine. (If you are unsure about masculine and feminine nouns, then review Chapter 21.) This usually means adding the feminine ending ة (*ta' marbuuTa*) to the adjective:

مُدَرِّس مَشْغول   (a) busy teacher [*masculine*]

مُدَرِّسة مَشْغولة   (a) busy teacher [*feminine*]

كِتاب ثَقيل   (a) heavy book [*masculine*]

حَقيبة ثَقيلة   (a) heavy bag [*feminine*]

All of the above examples are *indefinite* ("<u>a</u> busy teacher"). If you want to make them *definite* (<u>the</u> busy teacher) you have to add الـ (*al*) to both the noun <u>and</u> the adjective:

المُدَرِّس المَشْغول   the busy teacher

الكِتاب الثَقيل   the heavy book

الحَقيبة الثَقيلة   the heavy bag

There are a few adjectives to which you cannot add *taa' marbuuTa* to make the feminine. They have different feminine forms. The most important of these are the adjectives describing the primary colors:

| Color | Masculine | Feminine |
|-------|-----------|----------|
| red | أَحْمَر ('aHmar) | حَمْراء (Hamraa') |
| blue | أَزْرَق ('azraq) | زَرْقاء (zarqaa') |
| yellow | أَصْفَر ('aSfar) | صَفْراء (Safraa') |
| black | أَسْوَد ('aswad) | سَوْداء (sawdaa') |
| white | أَبْيَض ('abyaD) | بَيْضاء (bayDaa') |
| green | أَخْضَر ('akhDar) | خَضْراء (khaDraa') |

# Adjectives with plurals

Adjectives also have a different plural form, but it is very important to remember that these will only be used with people. Nonhumans (things, ideas, etc.) use <u>feminine singular</u> adjectives.

Many adjectives begin with مُ (*mu*) and are participles of the derived forms of the verb (see Chapter 16). These can be made plural by adding ـونَ (*uuna*) for males and ـات (*aat*) for females, but others have their own particular plurals. It is best to check in a dictionary, which will give the plural after the adjective. Here are some examples of adjectives used with humans and nonhuman plurals so that you can compare them. For a more complete overview of the plural in general, see Chapter 25.

ظُروف مُناسَبة   suitable circumstances

مُوَظَّفونَ مُناسَبونَ   suitable [male] employees

مُوَظَّفات مُناسَبات   suitable [female] employees

كُتُب جَديدة   new books

مُدَرِّسونَ جُدُد   new [male] teachers

# Comparatives

If you want to compare two things, you will need to use the comparative form of the adjective. The rules for forming the comparative are similar to English.

### Comparatives with simple adjectives

In English, we put "-er" on the end of short words to make a comparative: "long*er*/short*er*/rich*er*/poor*er*," etc. In Arabic, the root letters of a simple adjective are put into the pattern أَفْعَل (*'afal*) to make a comparative:

كَبير (*kabiir*) big → أَكْبَر (*'akbar*) bigger

قَصير (*qaSiir*) short → أَقْصَر (*'aqSar*) shorter

لَطيف (*laTiif*) gentle → أَلْطَف (*'alTaf*) gentler

If an adjective has a doubled root, they are written together. If it ends in a و (*waaw*) or a ي (*yaa'*), this becomes an *'alif maqSuura* (*yaa'* with no dots pronounced *aa*):

جَديد (*jadiid*) new → أَجَدّ (*'ajadd*) newer

ذَكِيّ (*dhakiiy*) clever → أَذْكَى (*'dhkaa*) cleverer

The equivalent of the English "than," as in "better <u>than</u>," is the Arabic

word مِنْ (*min*). You will most often find the comparative used in this
way. It does <u>not</u> change depending on whether the word it is describing
is masculine or feminine:

أَخِي أَقْصَر مِن أُخْتِي.   My brother is shorter than my sister.

القاهِرة أَكْبَر مِنْ الخَرْطوم.   Cairo is bigger than Khartoum.

If you add الـ (*al*) to a comparative, the meaning becomes *superlative*
the equivalent of the English "-est", as in "bigg<u>est</u>, short<u>est</u>," etc.:

أَخِي هُوَ الأَقْصَر في العائلة.   My brother [he] is the shortest in the family.

طائرة كونْكورْد هِيَ الأَسْرَع.   The Concord airplane [it] is the fastest.

## Comparatives with longer adjectives

In English, when we have a long adjective we want to make
comparative, we use the word "more" (or "less"), rather than putting
"-er" on the end: "<u>more</u> comfortable/<u>more</u> suitable/<u>less</u> adaptable."

Arabic is similar. The word أَكْثَر (*'akthar* – "more") or
أَقَلّ (*'aqall* – "less") is added in front of the <u>noun</u> to make the
comparative:

أَكْثَر مُلائمة   more suitable

أَكْثَر اِحْتِراماً   more respected

أَقَلّ اِسْتِعْمالاً   less utilized

*Note:* The nouns are now in the accusative case (*mulaa'amatan,* etc.) — see Appendix (ii).

# 24 Describing position (prepositions of place)

Words used to describe the position of something, such as the English "on/in/above/below/opposite," etc., are called *prepositions of place*. Here are some of the most common:

عَلَى (ع*alaa*) on

في (*fii*) in

إلَى (*'ilaa*) to(ward)

فَوْقَ (*fawqa*) above

تَحْتَ (*taHta*) under

أمـام (*'amaama*) in front of

وَراءَ (*waraa'a*) behind

بَيْن (*bayna*) between

حَوْلَ (*Hawla*) around

مَعَ (*ma*ع*a*) with

بِجانِب (*bijaanib*) next to

عِنْدَ (ع*inda*) with (someone), "chez"

Examples:

المَلَفّ تَحْت المَكْتَب.
The file is under the desk.

المُدير العامّ عَنْدَ عَميل اليَوْم.
The general manager is with a client today.

ذَهَبْتُ إلَى البَنْك أمْس.
I went to the bank yesterday.

وَجَدْتُ صَديقي وَراءَ البَيْت في الحَديقة.
I found my friend behind the house in the garden.

هَلْ رَأَيْتَ نَظارتي عَلَى البيانو؟
Did you see my glasses on the piano?

# 25 Plurals

In English, plurals are words referring to <u>more than one</u> thing and are generally formed by adding the letter -*s*: book<u>s</u>, idea<u>s</u>, letter<u>s</u>, etc. There are some words to which you have to add -*es* – box<u>es</u>, church<u>es</u> – and a few isolated irregularities, such as "man" becoming "men."

In Arabic, plurals refer to <u>more than two</u> things. The dual form is used for two (see Chapter 28.) In addition, most plurals are more like the English "man/men" example than a case of simply adding letters on the end of a word.

The area of plurals is one of the few genuinely complicated in basic Arabic grammar. This chapter will give you the essentials, but be prepared to learn each plural individually with the singular.

## Forming plurals

Learning how to form the plural for Arabic words is a long and sometimes frustrating business. However, if you persevere, you will eventually learn most of the common plurals and acquire an instinct for the others.

### Sound plurals

All plurals are classified as either *sound* or *broken*. Sound plurals are the simplest to learn but unfortunately have limitations in how widely they are used. There are two sound plurals:

*Masculine*: formed by adding ـُونَ (-*uuna**) on the end of the singular and used mainly (but not exclusively) for male professions:

مُدَرِّس (*mudarris*) teacher → مُدَرِّسُونَ (*mudarrisuuna*) teachers

نَجّار (*najjaar*) carpenter → نَجّارُونَ (*najjaaruuna*) carpenters

* Changes to ـِينَ (-*iina*) in the accusative and genitive case — see Appendix (ii).

*Feminine*: formed by adding ـات (-*aat*) on the end of the singular. If the word ends in a *taa' marbuuTa* (ة), this must be removed first. Like its masculine equivalent, the sound feminine plural is used for professions but is also used for a number of other words, especially verbal nouns from the derived forms (see Chapter 16.)

مُدَرِّسة (*mudarrisa*) teacher [*fem.*] → مُدَرِّسات (*mudarrisaat*) teachers

اِجْتِماع (*ijtimaaع*) meeting → اِجْتِماعَات (*ijtimaaعaat*) meetings

اِصْلاح (*iSlaaH*) reform → اِصْلاحَات (*iSlaaHaat*) reforms

## Broken plurals

The majority of plurals are broken plurals, so called because the singular is broken apart and different long and short vowels are arranged around the root letters. Look at this example of how the plural of the word وَلَد (*walad* – boy) is formed:

 *singular:*

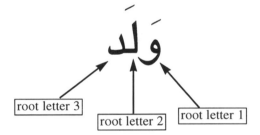

 *plural:*

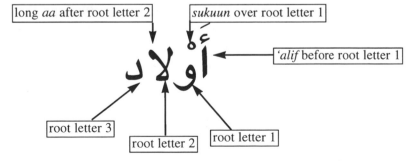

This plural pattern is the أَفْعال (*'afaal*) pattern, with the letters *faa'* (ف), *عain* (ع), and *lam* (ل) representing the three root letters. There are many different plural patterns, but some are much more common than others. It does not matter how the singular is vowelized, the plural pattern will always be the same, except that you have to know which to use!

Here are the eight of the most common patterns with examples.

| Pattern | Example plural | Singular of... |
|---|---|---|
| أَفْعَال (*'afعaal*) | أَقْلَام (*'aqlaam*) | قَلَم (*qalam:* pen) |
| فُعُول (*fuعuul*) | بُيُوت (*buyuut*) | بَيْت (*bayt:* house) |
| فِعَال (*fiعaal*) | كِلَاب (*kilaab*) | كَلْب (*kalb:* dog) |
| فُعُل (*fuعul*) | كُتُب (*kutub*) | كِتَاب (*kitaab:* book) |
| فُعَل (*fuعal*) | دُوَل (*duwal*) | دَوْلة (*dawla:* country) |
| أَفْعُل (*'afعul*) | أَشْهُر (*'ashhur*) | شَهْر (*shahr:* month) |
| فُعَلَاء (*fuعalaa'*) | وُزَرَاء (*wuzaraa'*) | وَزِير (*waziir:* minister) |
| أَفْعِلَاء (*'afعilaa'*) | أَصْدِقَاء (*'aSdiqaa'*) | صَدِيق (*Sadiiq:* friend) |

You will have to look in a dictionary to find which pattern to use for an individual word. The plural will be given after the singular.

# Human and nonhuman plurals

Arabic grammar has two different categories of plural: human (e.g. "men," "nurses," etc.) and nonhuman (e.g., "books," "negotiations," etc.). This distinction is <u>very</u> important to remember. ***The masculine and feminine plural forms of verbs, adjectives, etc. are only used with human plural nouns. Nonhuman plurals are regarded as feminine singular.*** So, for example, the plural كُتُب (*kutub* – books) would be referred to as هي (*hiya* – she) and <u>not</u> هُم (*hum* – they), and would be described as جَدِيدة (*jadiida* – new [*fem. singular*]) and <u>not</u> جُدُد (*judud* – new [*masc. plural*]):

هذِهِ هِيَ الكُتُب الجَدِيدة.   These are the new books.

إنْتَهَت المُنَاقَشات أمْس.   The discussions ended (*intahat* – fem. sing.) yesterday.

You need to etch this concept into your brain! Look back at the verb chapters and remind yourself of the feminine singular verbs. You could practice by forming a few sentences using nonhuman plurals.

# 26 Describing possession

## إضافة (*'iDaafa*)

In English, we have two main ways of describing possession – using the word "of," or the possessive " -'s ":

the client's office

the office of the client

The most common way of describing possession in Arabic is closer to the second example above, in that the word for "office" would come first followed by the word for "client." The difference is that the two words are put directly together (the meaning "of" is understood) and only the last word can have the article الـ (*al*):

مكْتَب العَميل  the office of the client

بَيْت المُدَرِّس  the teacher's house

وَزير الاقْتِصاد  the minister of the economy

This structure, where two (or more) nouns are put back to back, is known as إضافة (*'iDaafa*), which literally means "addition." Nothing can come between two words in an *'iDaafa*. So if you want to add an adjective, it must come right at the end and will have the article الـ (*al*):

مكْتَب العَميل المُرْتَفِع  the elevated office of the client

بَيْت المُدَرِّس الفَخْم  the teacher's luxurious house

وَزير الاقْتِصاد المِصْريّ  the Egyptian minister of the economy

Watch out for the *sound masculine plural* and the *dual* when they are the first noun in an *'iDaafa*. They lose the final *nuun* (ن):

مُدَرِّسون teachers → مُدَرِّسو* المَدْرسة  the teachers of the school

مُدَرِّسان 2 teachers → مُدَرِّسا** المَدْرسة  the two teachers of the school

\* Changes to ي (*-ii*) in the accusative and genitive case — see Appendix (ii).

\*\* Changes to يَ (*-ay*) in the accusative and genitive case – see Appendix (ii).

The *taa' marbuuTa* on the end of most feminine nouns is pronounced when the word is the first in the *'iDaafa*:

مَدينة لُنْدُن (*madiinat lundun*) the city of London

# Possessive (attached) pronouns

Possessive pronouns are the equivalent of the English "my," "his," "ours," etc. In Arabic they are <u>joined to the end</u> of the word and are also known as *attached pronouns*:

مَكْتَبنا (*maktabnaa*) <u>our</u> office

بَيتي (*baytii*) <u>my</u> house

Here is a table of the possessive pronouns with the example showing the ending on the word بيت (*bayt* – house):

|  |  | Possessive ending | Example |
|---|---|---|---|
| أنا | I | ـِي (ii)** | بَيتي (baytii) |
| أنْتَ | you (masc.) | كَ (ka) | بَيتُكَ (bayt[u*]ka) |
| أنْتِ | you (fem.) | كِ (ki) | بَيتُكِ (bayt[u]ki) |
| هُوَ | he/it | ـهُ (hu) | بَيتهُ (bayt[u]hu) |
| هِيَ | she/it | ـهَا (haa) | بَيتُها (bayt[u]haa) |
| نَحْنُ | we | ـنَا (naa) | بَيتُنا (bayt[u]naa) |
| أنْتُمْ | you (masc. pl.) | كُمْ (kum) | بَيتُكُمْ (bayt[u]kum) |
| أنتُنَّ | you (fem. pl.) | كُنَّ (kunna) | بَيتُكُنَّ (bayt[u]kunna) |
| هُم | they (masc. pl.) | ـهُمْ (hum) | بَيتُهُمْ (bayt[u]hum) |
| هُنَّ | they (fem. pl.) | ـهُنَّ (hunna) | بَيتُهُنَّ (bayt[u]hunna) |

**Notes to the table:**

* The additional *Damma* (ُ [u]) is the nominative case ending, which can change to *fatHa* or *kasra* – see Appendix (ii). Note that the endings ـه (*hu*) and هم (*hum*) become ـه (*hi*) and هم (*him*) if this additional vowel is a *kasra*: بيته/بيتهم (*baytihi/baytihim*).

** The *ii* ending changes to *ya* if the word finishes in a long vowel: محامي (*muHaamiiya* – my attorney)

Attached pronouns can also be used with verbs, prepositions, and words such as أنّ (*'anna* – that).

## Attached pronouns with verbs

You can add the pronouns in the table opposite to verbs, except that the ending ـي (*ii*) changes to ـني (*nii*). Otherwise the endings are the same:

ضَرَبْتُها.   I hit her.

باعوه أمْس.   They sold it yesterday.

تَزورنا كُلَّ أُسْبوع.   She visits us every week.

## Attached pronouns with prepositions and أنّ

The attached pronouns can also be put on prepositions (see Chapter 24 for examples of prepositions) and word such as أنّ.

Note that the *nuun* of the preposition مِن (*min* – from) is doubled when *ii* is added:

أَخَذَتْ أُمّي فُلوسي مِنّي.   My mother took my money from me.

The word أنّ is pronounced *'anna* before an attached pronoun (or noun), except for أنّي (*'annii* – "that I"):

ذَكَرَتْ أَنَّها تَحْتاج إلَيْها.   She mentioned that she needed it.

شَكَوْتُ أَنّي مُفْلِس.   I complained that I was broke.

# 27 Questions and relative clauses

## Questions

Questions are straightforward in Arabic. There is no special form of the verb used with questions. Simple questions can be formed by adding a question mark to the end of a sentence or by putting the word هَلْ (*hal*), or less often أ (*'a*), in front of it:

هذا كِتاب. This is a book.

هَلْ هذا كِتاب؟/ أهذا كِتاب؟/ هذا كِتاب؟ Is this a book?

Other questions are formed by using the appropriate question word:

أَيْنَ البَنْك؟ **Where** is the bank?      مَتَى نَذْهَب؟ **When** are we going?

ماذا* تَفْعَل؟ **What** are you doing?      مَنْ وَجَدَ المِفْتاح؟ **Who** found the key?

ما* اسْمُكَ؟ **What** is your name?      لِماذا تَصيح؟ **Why** are you shouting?

كَيْف أُمُّكَ؟ **How** is your mother?      بِكَم الآلة؟ **How much** is the machine?

\* *maadhaa* is followed by a verb, *maa* by a noun.

## Relative clauses

The Arabic relative pronouns ("which/who") are:

اَلَّذي (*aladhii*) [*masculine sing.*]      اَلَّذينَ (*aladhiina*) [*masculine pl.*]
اَلَّتي (*alatii*) [*feminine sing.*]      اَللاتي (*allaatii*) [*feminine pl.*]

Pay particular attention to the difference between these two clauses:

الوَلَد الذي ضَرَبَ المُدَرِّس the boy who hit the teacher
الوَلَد الذي ضَرَبَهُ المُدَرِّس the boy whom the teacher hit [<u>him</u>]

If the second sentence is indefinite, the relative pronoun is left out:

وَلَد ضَرَبَهُ المُدَرِّس a boy whom the teacher hit [him]

# 28 The dual

Arabic has a separate form for talking about two things: the *dual* form. This is less common than the *singular* (one thing) or the *plural* (three or more things), and for this reason it has been separated from the main chapters. Having said that, you will come across the dual sometimes and may have to use it occasionally, so you need to know the basics of how it works.

The dual in general is characterized by a long *aa*. Look at the dual words for "you" and "they:"

أَنْتُما (*'antumaa*) you two [*masculine* and *feminine* ]

هُما (*humaa*) they two [*masculine* and *feminine* ]

If you want to refer to two people or things (*nouns*), you add the dual ending ان (*aani*). (This ending changes to ـَين (*-ayni*) in the accusative and genitive case — see Appendix (ii).) If the nouns end with *taa' marbuuTa*, this is fully pronounced when you add the ending:

كِتاب (*kitaab*) book ➙ كِتابان (*kitaabaani*) two books

مَدينة (*madiina*) city ➙ مَدينتان (*madiinataani*) two cities

The dual ending is also added to adjectives:

هُما مَشْغولان. They (two) are busy.

هُناكَ مُمَرِّضَتان جَديدتان في المُسْتَشْفَى.
There are two new nurses in the hospital.

There are also special verb endings for the dual. You can find these in Chapter 17.

# Appendixes

# Appendix (i)
# Guide to pronunciation/transliteration

Here are the Arabic consonants, vowels and dipthongs, with the transliteration used in this book and pronunciation tips ([S] = sun letter, see pages 105–6).

## consonants:

ب (baa') *b*, as in "bat"

ت (taa') *t*, as in "tank" [S]

ث (thaa') *th*, as in "this" [S]

ج (jiim) *j*, as in "jelly"

ح (Haa') *H*, strong breathy *h*

خ (khaa') *kh*, as in Scottish "loch"

د (daal) *d*, as in "dad" [S]

ذ (dhaal) *dh*, as in "that" [S]

ر (raa') *r*, as in "rain" [S]

ز (zay) *z*, as in "zero" [S]

س (siin) *s*, as in "sorry" [S]

ش (shiin) *sh*, as in "shut" [S]

ص (Saad) *S*, strong, emphatic *s* [S]

ض (Daad) *D*, strong, emphatic *d* [S]

ط (Taa') *T*, strong, emphatic *t* [S]

ظ (Zaa') *Z*, strong, emphatic *z* [S]

ع (ᶜayn) ᶜ, guttural stop

غ (ghayn) *gh*, as in French "maigret"

ف (faa') *f*, as in "fall"

ق (qaaf) *q*, said from back of throat

ك (kaaf) *k*, as in "kate"

ل (laam) *l*, as in "letter"

م (miim) *m*, as in "met"

ن (nuun) *n*, as in "never" [S]

ه (haa') *h*, as in "hand"

و (waaw) *w*, as in "wand"

ي (yaa') *y*, as in "yellow"

ء (hamza) ', short pause/stop [1]

## short vowels:

َ (fatHa) *a*, as in "mat"

ُ (Damma) *u*, as in "sugar"

ِ (kasra) *i*, as in "bit"

## long vowels:

ا aa, as in "far" [2]

ُو uu, as in "boot"

ِي ii, as in "meet"

## dipthongs:

َو aw, as in "how" or "home"

َي ay, as in "lie"

(1) Note that that there is a special type of *hamza* found at the beginning of the word *al* ("the") and a few other words. This is called *hamza al-waSl* ("the joining hamza"). It is not usually written and the vowel it carries elides when preceded by another vowel: الْبَيْت (al-bayt – "the house") but وَجَدوا الْبَيْت (wajaduu l-bayt – "they found the house")

(2) Occasionally, *aa* is written using a *yaa'* (without dots) rather than an *'alif*. This always happens at the end of a word and is called *'alif maqsuura*: صَحْرَى (SaHraa– "desert").

# Appendix (ii)
# Grammatical case endings

Many languages — German, for example — have grammatical cases
that affect the noun endings. Arabic has three cases — nominative,
accusative and genitive. However, the case endings are not usually
pronounced in Modern Arabic, nor do they generally affect the
spelling. Situations where you might hear them include high-level
academic discussions (on TV, for example), recitations of the Quran or
other religious and literary texts, or sometimes as a kind of flourish at
the end of a sentence. Most beginning and intermediate learners can
gloss over this aspect of Arabic grammar. However, it is useful to
know that these cases exist and to have some idea of how they work so
you are not thrown when you do meet them.

The following table shows how the three cases work for most nouns in
the definite and indefinite. The underlining shows the case ending. The
ending in bold— the extra accusative *'alif* — affects the basic spelling
and you should try to remember this.

|  | nominative | accusative | genitive |
|---|---|---|---|
| indefinite | بيتٌ *(baytun)* | بيتاً *(baytan)* | بيتٍ *(baytin)* |
| definite | البيتُ *(al-baytu)* | البيتَ *(al-bayta)* | البيتِ *(al-bayti)* |

The most important uses of the cases are listed below, but this is just an
indication. For more information, consult a detailed Arabic grammar book.
- *nominative*: for the subject of a sentence
- *accusative*: for the object of a verb
- *genitive*: after prepositions
        for the second noun in an *'idafa* (see page 119)

There are exceptions to the endings given above. The most common of
these is the sound masculine plural:

|  | nominative | accusative | genitive |
|---|---|---|---|
| indefinite | مُدَرِسونَ *(mudarrisuuna)* | مُدَرِسونَ *(mudarrisiina)* | مُدَرِسونَ *(mudarrisiina)* |
| definite* | المُدَرِسونَ *(al-mudarrisuuna)* | المُدَرِسونَ *(al-mudarrisiina)* | المُدَرِسونَ *(al-mudarrisiina)* |

* The final *nuun* is dropped in an *'idaafa* construction — see page 119.

# Appendix (iii)   Numbers

Here are the Arabic numbers, as numerals and spelled out. Arabic numbers are complex. The most important aspects are noted at the bottom of the page, but you will need a full grammar book to cover all the idiosyncrasies.

واحِد ١ (waaHid) – 1

إِثْنان ٢ (ithnaan) – 2

ثلاثة ٣ (thalaatha) – 3

أرْبَعة ٤ ('arbaعa) – 4

خَمْسة ٥ (khamsa) – 5

سِتّة ٦ (sitta) – 6

سَبْعة ٧ (sabعa) – 7

ثَمانية ٨ (thamaaniya) – 8

تِسْعة ٩ (tisعa) – 9

عَشَرة ١٠ (عashara) – 10

أحَد عَشَر ١١ ('ahad عashar) – 11

إثْنا عَشَر ١٢ (ithnaa عashar) – 12

ثَلاثة عَشَر ١٣ (thalaathat عashar) – 13

أرْبَعة عَشَر ١ ('arbaعat عashar) – 14

خَمْسة عَشَر ١٥ (khamsat عashar) – 15

سِتّة عَشَر ١٦ (sittat عashar) – 16

سَبْعة عَشَر ١٧ (sabعat عashar) – 17

ثَمانية عَشَر ١٨ (thamaaniyat عashar) – 18

تِسْعة عَشَر ١٩ (tisعat عashar ) – 19

عِشْرون ٢٠ (عishruun) – 20

واحِد وَعِشْرون ٢١ (waaHid wa عishruun) – 21

إِثْنان وَعِشْرون ٢٢ (ithnaan wa عishruun) – 22

ثَلاثون ٣٠ (thalaathuun) – 30

أرْبَعون ٤٠ ('arbaعuun) – 40

خَمْسون ٥٠ (khamsuun) – 50

سِتّون ٦٠ (sittuun) – 60

سَبْعون ٧٠ (sabعuun) – 70

ثَمانون ٨٠ (thamaanuun) – 80

تِسْعون ٩٠ (tisعuun) – 90

مِئة ١٠٠ (mi'a) – 100

ألْف ١٠٠٠ ('alf) – 1,000

مِلْيون ١٠٠٠٠٠٠ (milyuun) – 1,000,000

**Note:**

• Arabic numerals are written left to right (see above).
• The numbers above are those you will meet most often. However, there are some changes if followed by a *feminine* noun, notably the numbers 3–9 will lose the ة (taa' marbuuta): ثلاث بَنات 3 girls; ثلاثة أوْلاد 3 boys;
• Numbers 3–9 are followed by a *plural* noun, but 11 upwards by a *singular* noun (in the accusative — see Appendix (ii): ثلاثون كِتابا 30 books; ثلاثة كُتُب 3 books;